THE
IMAGINATIVE WORLD
OF THE
REFORMATION

THE
IMAGINATIVE WORLD
OF THE
REFORMATION

PETER MATHESON

FORTRESS PRESS   MINNEAPOLIS

THE IMAGINATIVE WORLD OF THE REFORMATION

First Fortress Press edition, 2001

ISBN 0–8006–3291–5

Printed and bound in Great Britain
by MPG Books Ltd, Bodmin, Cornwall   AF 1–3291

05   04   03   02   01   1   2   3   4   5   6   7   8   9   10

*To my father, James,
and to the memory of my mother, Janet*

Heinrich Vogtherr, the Younger. The Fool

CONTENTS

ILLUSTRATIONS

ABBREVIATIONS

AvG   Peter Matheson, tr. and ed., *Argula von Grumbach: A Woman's Voice in the Reformation*. T. & T. Clark: Edinburgh, 1995.

CR   C. G. Bretschneider, ed., *Corpus Reformatorum. Melanchthons Opera*. Halle, 1834ff.

CW   Peter Matheson, tr. and ed., *The Collected Works of Thomas Müntzer*. T. & T. Clark: Edinburgh, 1988.

LW   *Luther's Works* (the 'American Luther'), eds. J. Pelikan and W. Lehman. 44 Vols. Concordia: Philadelphia and St Louis, 1955ff.

MSB   *Thomas Müntzer: Schriften und Briefe*. In collaboration with Paul Kirn edited by Gunther Franz (Quellen und Forschungen zur Reformationsgeschichte, Vol. XXXIII) Gerd Mohn: Gutersloh, 1968.

W   *D. Martin Luther's Works*. Kritische Gesamtausgabe. Weimar, 1883ff.

WBr   *Briefwechsel*, 1933ff.

PREFACE

This book had its genesis in the invitation by the Divinity Faculty of Edinburgh to give a series of Gunning Lectures in 1998. This gave me the opportunity to develop the theme of imagination in the Reformation. My heartfelt thanks are due to New College for its extraordinarily kind hospitality and encouragement during my time there. My debt to such New College luminaries as Professor John McIntyre and Principal Ruth Page for their pioneering work in the relationship between theology and imagination will also be obvious.

Moreover, my fascination with church history grew from the notable example of Professor Alec Cheyne in my student days at New College, and later when I was a junior colleague of his. It is a pleasure to record my gratitude to him here. I have sought to retain something of the immediacy of the oral delivery of the lectures in preparing them for publication.

I would also like to take this chance to thank Dr Geoffrey Green, of T&T Clark, for his support and friendship over some twenty years, and to his staff. As always, responsibility for the final product remains mine.

Warm thanks for permission to reproduce documents and illustrations is given to: the Bayerisches Haupstaatsarchiv, Munich; the Gothaer Kultur- und Fremdenverkehrsbetrieb Schlossmuseum, Gotha; the Thüringer Museum, Eisenach.

PETER MATHESON

CHAPTER ONE

THE STIRRING OF THE IMAGINATION

The Reformation has become a conundrum to most of us, almost an embarrassment. This is surprising and paradoxical. The historiography of the Reformation has probably never been more creative, lively and controversial than it is today – and I hope to give some glimpses of this in these chapters. However, outside the charmed world of Church or Academy, the Reformation is viewed in almost exclusively negative terms. The most urgent concerns of the Reformers – justification by faith, the sole authority of Scripture – have become a closed book to most of us these days and are viewed with bemused bafflement. The doctrinal archaeologists, busily unearthing layer after layer of controversy about the sacraments or shifts in the understanding of grace, have left most folk, even in the Church, far behind. We can uncover the history of the Reformation, but cannot recover its meaning. Perhaps it is not unconnected with this that Protestantism itself appears, in the Western world at least, to have reached its sell-by date and, to judge by the pronouncements of media pundits, is being reduced to clear.

The central thesis of this book is that a quite new approach to the Reformation may be required. Our current tendency towards a doctrinal approach on the one hand and to social reductionism on the other has led us into a blind alley. These chapters will suggest shifting the focus to the imaginative world of the Reformation, with a particular interest in the early German Reformation, or rather Reformations.

For we can no longer think in terms of one, presumably Lutheran, Reformation. Humanist, communal, Lutheran, radical, reformed variants, not to mention Catholic, all jostled alongside one another. Nor was there one Germany. The picturesque, wooded valleys of the south west are another universe from the great fertile plains of the north east, or the rich channels of the Rhine and the Danube. There is a civic and a rural, a Franconian and a Rhenish, a Saxon and a Swabian Germany, and their imaginations differ as much as their dialects.[1] At the same time, no small part of the fascination of this period is that humanism, evangelicalism and peasant revolt at times appeared to be on the verge of weaving these disparate realms together into a common dream, the dream of a revived, restored, reformed German nation.

We come with our own urgent and specific questions about the reach of the religious imagination. Edwin Muir, too little known these days, has described our lives as a mysterious fable in which 'we receive more than we can ever give; we receive it from the past, on which we draw with every breath, but also . . . from the Source of the mystery itself, which religious people call Grace'. Fabulous, mysterious, gratuitous. Not a bad description of life! He describes the effect on him of a little plaque representing the Annunciation in the Via degli Artisti in Rome; on it, an angel and a young girl are inclined towards one another, their knees bent as if in love, '*tutto tremante*'. For Edwin Muir the perfect symbol of a Christ born in the flesh. Why is it, he asks, that while such imagery abounds in Catholicism, we Protestants appear content with an impoverished imagination, which he indelicately, but not so inaccurately, dubs, 'the odour of ancient Bibles'.[2]

---

[1]   Miriam Usher Chrisman, *Conflicting Visions of Reform. German Lay Propaganda Pamphlets, 1519–1530* (Atlantic Highlands, NJ: Humanities Press, 1995), p. 11, points out that 30% of lay pamphleteers who could be traced came from the Rhenish Palatinate and Franconia; another 20% from Swabia, centred on Nuremberg, Augsburg, Reutlingen; and only 18% in the two Saxonies. Lay pamphleteers were mainly in SW Germany, Franconia, Alsace and the Rhenish Palatinate.

[2]   *An Autobiography* (London: Hogarth Press, 1954), pp. 281, 277f.

An impoverished imagination? What was it that fired the Reformers? What was it that encouraged hundreds of thousands to follow them, abandoning the wealth of experience, piety, scholarship, churchmanship and indeed imagination which constituted the medieval Church, that whole multi-layered universe so movingly reconstructed for us in recent times by John Bossy, Eamonn Duffy, Christopher Haigh, Robert Whiting and others?[3] Fritz Wunderli, in his spirited book, *Peasant Fires*, on the shepherd preacher known to us as the 'Drummer of Niklashausen', describes the high feasts during the church year as the 'enchanted time'.[4] Why did people turn their back on such enchantment?

Does our current disillusionment with the Reformation rest on its departure from such enchantment, its character as a iconoclastic splurge? Was it, as Peter Burke suggests, a lenten puritanical pruning by a high-minded élite, the state-builders, clerics and bourgeois fathers who for the sake of education and social discipline curbed not only the pleasures of the multitude, but the more sophisticated celebration of liminality?[5] This thesis of a disjunction between popular and élite religion has found little favour of late, as it appears to ride roughshod over too many awkward realities.

Or was the Reformation fired by a different way of imagining, something more akin, perhaps, to the fierce outrage and merciless eye of the Marxist dramatist Bertolt Brecht in this century, who stripped the theatre of its magic in order to provoke and empower

---

[3] John Bossy, *Christianity in the West. 1400–1700* (Oxford: Oxford University Press, 1985); Eamonn Duffy, *The Stripping of the Altars: Traditional Religion in England c. 1400–1580* (New Haven and London: Yale University Press, 1992); Christopher Haigh, *Reformation and Resistance in Tudor Lancashire* (London: Cambridge University Press, 1975); Robert Whiting, *The Blind Devotion of the People: Popular Religion and the English Reformation* (Cambridge: Cambridge University Press, 1989)..

[4] *Peasant Fires: the Drummer of Niklashausen* (Bloomington, IN: Indiana University Press, 1992).

[5] Peter Burke, *Popular Culture in Early Modern Europe* (Aldershot: Scolar Press, 1994).

the audience into action? Brecht talked of *Verfremdung*, making the familiar alien. Did the Reformers deploy the imagination in this way? After all, the radical preacher and liturgist, Thomas Müntzer, described the Mass as theatre, as that 'papal black magic, like the incantations used to conjure up the devil', and wrote the first vernacular German Mass to replace it.[6]

Or are these questions wrongly put? Did people follow the Reformers, or was the Reformation itself, as some have argued, a uniquely communitarian event in European history? Was it rooted in popular and populist traditions, which surfaced in art, poetry, song, pamphlet and that revolution of the common folk we have traditionally called the Peasants' War? What were the hidden springs of imagination, high up in the hills, that were to feed the broad river of the Reformation?

Previous generations have explained the success of the Reformation in moralistic terms, as a reaction against the corruption of the late medieval Church, or in institutional terms, as a structural reform to meet the needs of the modern nation–state. It has been hailed by others as the trail-blazer of a new spirituality or, by the Marxist historians we are now busy pretending never existed, as the first bourgeois revolution. And, of course, theologians and church historians tend to have seen it primarily, if not exclusively, in doctrinal terms, as a theological initiative based on the formal norm of *sola Scriptura* and the material norm of justification by faith.

It would be a brave or foolish person who discounted any of these factors. The approach of these chapters, however, will be different. While not ignoring the doctrinal or structural innovations introduced by the Reformation (how could we?), they will focus our attention on the imaginative leap which underlay them.

Let us illustrate what is meant by this. A dramatic 'happening' took place on the streets of Bern during Lent in 1522. On one

---

[6]   *The Collected Works of Thomas Müntzer* (tr. and ed. Peter Matheson; Edinburgh: T. & T. Clark, 1988 = CW), pp. 181, 174.

side of an alley appeared 'Christ' with his crown of thorns, riding on a donkey and surrounded by a swarm of poor, blind followers. On the other side rode a martial three-crowned 'pope' surrounded by a pompous procession of cavalry and footmen, drums and trumpets. The peasants crowding around asked: 'Who rides there so humbly?' 'Who is that great Emperor?' The answers given them provoked, according to the 1525 pamphlet which described all this, a predictable explosion of anger as the common folk realised that they were being fleeced of their money by the pope. Insult was added to injury by the money being used to hire Swiss mercenaries for Rome's dubious political campaigns. On the other hand, however, there was a realisation by the peasant onlookers that the humble rider on the donkey was 'our highest treasure, sweet, mild, and merciful, the eternal father's word, who has invited us [poor folk] to the heavenly supper in the highest king's hall'.[7] Behind both the anticlericalism and the adoration of the Christ lay formidable transformations in patterns of deference, concepts of honour and hidden assumptions.

Alfred North Whitehead suggests that to understand the spirit of an era one should look less at the intellectual systems explicitly defended by its exponents than at their unconscious presuppositions.[8] We have also become accustomed recently to Thomas Kuhn's suggestion that the world of science progresses through radical shifts in the root metaphors of an age, its so-called paradigms: the habits of mind and method which are so engrained that we are not even conscious of them. It has been suggested that Luther's theological language, with its concern to be biblical, to

[7]   Niklaus Manuel, *Ein Fassnacht spyl/ so zu Bernn uff/ der Herren Fassnacht in den M.D. XXII./ jar/ von burgers sünen gemacht ist . . .* Fiche 938/2345, 1525; cf. the recent assessment of his work by Bruce Gordon, 'Toleration in the early Swiss Reformation: the art and politics of Niklaus Manuel of Berne', in *Tolerance and Intolerance in the European Reformation*, ed. Ole Peter Grell and Bob Scribner (Cambridge: Cambridge University Press, 1996), pp. 128–44.

[8]   *Science and the Modern World* (New York: New American Library, 1948), pp. 49–50.

follow 'the grammar of the Holy Spirit', is best understood as a 'modified interaction metaphor', which allowed heavenly things to be articulated through the clash of earthly categories.[9] The Bern 'happening' may best be explained in a similar way.

Much of my own recent work has been devoted to the popular literature of the Reformation and the intricate and alluring tapestry of its forms, conventions, tropes and language.[10] This has suggested to me that the reforming process was not fundamentally about ideas in the mind or structures in church and state but indicated much more elemental changes in spiritual direction. These are signposted by the creative metaphors of the preachers and teachers, the images in literature and art, the rhythms and melodies of the popular ballads and chorales which sang the Reformation into people's souls.

We are quite rightly impressed by the iconoclastic dimensions of the Reformation, the pruning of the liturgies and the decimation of the saints' days, the removal of statues, paintings and even stained glass from the churches. But such iconoclasm may be eclipsed by what we can call the iconopoiac energies of the Reformation, its creativity in producing new allegories and metaphors for the divine and the human which, by their novel connections and collocations, bedded together the hitherto incompatible and subverted one cosmos while paving the way for another. Metaphors which were largely drawn, as in Nicholas Manuel's play in Bern, from a reanimated, reactualised Bible. It may give pause for thought that the leading theorist of iconoclasm in the early Reformation, Andreas Karlstadt, dedicated his 1521 tract on the Eucharist to none other than Albrecht Dürer, the great humanist artist.[11]

---

[9]   Dennis Bielfeldt, 'Luther, Metaphor and Theological Language', *Modern Theology* 6:2 (1990), pp. 121–35.

[10]   *The Rhetoric of the Reformation* (Edinburgh: T. & T. Clark, 1998).

[11]   *The Essential Carlstadt. Fifteen tracts by Andreas Bodenstein (Carlstadt) from Karlstadt* (tr. and ed. E. J. Furcha; Waterloo, Ontario and Scottdale, PA: Herald Press, 1995), p. 40.

When your metaphors change, your world changes with them. As Lévi-Strauss has said, 'metaphors are based on an intuitive sense of the logical relations between one realm and other realms ... Metaphor, far from being a decoration that is added to language, purifies it and restores it to its original nature.'[12] This is intriguing and illuminating because purification and restoration, of course, come very close to what Luther and his followers meant by reformation. *Rain und pur*, clear and pure, are terms which surface a thousand times in the sermons, songs, poems and pamphlets which acclaim the new gospel.

Images, like people, can and do burn out. They have to be continually renewed, or rejigged. Perhaps what happened in the Reformation was that one imaginative architecture was replaced by another. The divine becomes more intimate, Christ as saviour rather than ominous judge; the human more earthy.[13] Every city becomes Jerusalem. The time is now and the place is here! A popular woodcut of the time showed John the Baptist welcoming Christ, but the river is not the Jordan; it is the River Pegnitz, with Nuremberg in the background.

Similarly an etching which portrays Luther and John Huss as co-celebrants of the Lord's Supper, although the latter had been martyred a century earlier, illustrates a totally new perspective. Lay people, personified in the Saxon princes, are being offered both bread and wine, while a fountain fed by blood from the wounds of Christ stands on the altar. The miraculous transformation of the elements is no longer central to the Mass; what excites wonder and awe now is the free

[12] Claude Lévi-Strauss, *The Raw and the Cooked. Introduction to a Science of Mythology*, 1 (tr. John and Doreen Weightman; London: Jonathan Cape, 1970), p. 339.

[13] Lionel Rothkrug makes the interesting point that the Reformation scored its greatest successes in the parts of Europe, namely northern Germany, with the fewest indigenous saints. *Religious Practices and Collective Perceptions: Hidden Homologies in the Renaissance and Reformation* (*Historical Reflections*, vol. 7, 1980).

forgiveness of sins.[14] Biblical images are being reworked here, released and unleashed to emphasise gratuity, access, intimacy. From this perspective the Reformation can be seen as an infinitely varied, but coherent and extended, metaphor for the bountifulness of God's grace.

If, however, there is anything to be said for this argument, then we are going to have to look in quite a new way at Protestantism, which – we have generally been encouraged to believe – is inimical to the imagination. The most powerful imaginations, Hugo von Hoffmanstal has said, are always conservative, for it is tradition which nourishes enchantment. When it disappears, all we are left with is the bald shape of reality.[15] Conversely, Newman adumbrates the views of a whole clutch of modern revisionists when he suggests, in his *Essay on Development*, that 'to be deep in history is to cease to be a Protestant'.[16] The stubborn evidence of reality would seem to refute that. None of the Reformers was without a keen sense of history. The question, perhaps, is how they saw it. Not romantically, for sure.

Indeed, the notable success of medieval historians of piety in uncovering for us the imaginative world of the pilgrimage, the social miracle of the Mass, the kinship patterns of the cult of saints, the intercourse between the living and the dead, should spur us on to attempt the same for the Reformation.[17] As we seek to do

---

[14]   The woodcut dates from 1559; the allegorical depiction of the Eucharist *c.* 1551; cf. *Reformation in Nürnberg. Umbruch und Bewahrung* (Schriften des Kunstpädagogischen Zentrums im Germanischen Nationalmuseum Nürnberg, 9; Nuremberg: Verlag Medien & Kultur, 1979), pp. 76f.

[15]   Quoted by Muir, *An Autobiography*, p. 220.

[16]   John Henry Newman, *An Essay on the Development of Christian Doctrine* (Harmondsworth: Penguin, 1974).

[17]   Some of these historians, particularly of late medieval England, have suggested that its rich, popular and variegated spirituality was replaced by Protestantism largely because of state-sponsored coercion or propaganda. This reductionist view has found only limited support. The recent death of Bob Scribner has robbed us of a scholar who preferred to talk of the Reformation replacing one imaginative cosmos by another. Of course there was state coercion

justice to the Reformers' imagination, we may find that traditional qualifiers such as 'conservative', 'liberal', 'radical' do not work.

It may be helpful to remember that the very term *reformatio*, which long preceded the Protestant reformation, was itself a visionary concept signifying much more than a list of demands, a programme. The very popular *Reformation of Emperor Sigismund*, which first appeared in 1439 but was frequently reprinted at the high point of the early Reformation around the year 1520, contained specific recommendations, such as an end to serfdom and the right of priests to marry, but it was above all a vision of a world in which reform would come from below, based on divine justice. People believed that a transformation of the whole world was imminent, a *voranderung der welt*, as Thomas Müntzer put it.[18] When interrogated after the battle of Frankenhausen in May 1525, the peasant leader, Heinrich Pfeiffer, declared that the common folk had 'wanted to make a Christian Reformation', by which he meant recasting the whole of social and political, as well as ecclesiastical, reality. One term often used by participants to describe the revolutionary events of 1524–5 was 'dance', 'joining the dance'. Reformation was less a shopping-list of demands than the choreography for a new dance.[19]

We shall, therefore, be asking in these chapters: What were the images which captured the popular imagination in the early years of the Reformation, which sent folk whirling? No one who remembers the scenes in Poland's shipyards as *Solidarnosc* took off, or around the Berlin Wall in 1989, will underestimate the importance of ordinary people finding their voice. People said at

---

in the Reformation period and of course magistrates used religion to control their citizens. But to resort to arguments about social control or patriarchy to explain all aspects of the Reformation is to explain it away. Important half-truths are the bane of good history.

[18]   Thomas Müntzer: *Schriften und Briefe* (ed. Günther Franz; Gütersloh: Gerd Mohn, 1968), pp. 420/26f.

[19]   *Quellen zur Geschichte des Bauernkrieges* (ed. Günther Franz; Darmstadt: Wiss Buchgeselleschaft, 1963), p. 536.

that time that a new language had been minted on the street. The truth, of course, was infinitely more complex. In the background had been the quiet, creative leadership by poets and pastors, activists and dreamers, little groups that had been meeting for years to pray and study and protest. From them flowed a fresh language of realism and hope; they provided much of the human leadership, the disciplines, the symbols, the songs. And in turn these acted as catalysts to spark off a thousand spontaneous initiatives: the flowers in the mouths of guns, whole seas of candles, the chants and slogans coined as people marched, the graffiti on the walls, the acts of peaceful defiance that toppled apparently invincible régimes. Something similar may have happened in the early Reformation.

In the remainder of this introductory chapter I shall look at the apocalyptic and anticlerical 'trailers' for this new landscape of the imagination. In subsequent chapters I shall seek to show how the 'new song' of the Reformation was sung, how it opened up a fresh, vernacular language, and created a public opinion for the first time in European history, a surge of informed consciousness independent of the authorities. Then the visionary dimensions in the rural and urban Reformation will be reviewed. Much of the most exciting research in recent times has been in this area. In the fourth chapter we shall address the ravaged, nightmarish landscape of cruelty, failure and despair, the dark side of the period, for nothing is less appropriate these days than an uncritical apologia for the Reformation. We shall then look, in the fifth chapter, at new research in the less studied areas of personal life. Finally, we shall look at the spirituality of the Reformation. All these areas are, of course, interrelated.

The Stirring of the Imagination

The phrase 'to stir the brew' was often used in the pamphlets of this period. The brew is the Church, society, life. The homely cooking analogy reflects an awareness of the complex mixture of ingredients in the pot, priests and people alike; but also that they

Unknown Nuremberg Artist c. *1530.*
Vision of the prophet Jeremiah, *Flugblätter, 39*

have to be disturbed, spooned out of place, swirled around, if the
eventual meal is to be a savoury one. We talk very similarly today
of people being 'stirrers'.

   The image is used frequently in Reformation writings in a
pejorative way. Jeremiah's menacing image of the boiling pot
portending imminent danger, which appears in many woodcuts,
may lurk in the background. Amidst the crisis of the Peasants'
War in May 1525, Luther talked of the devil sensing that the Last
Day was at hand and stirring up the dregs in the pot.[20] His
opponent Thomas Müntzer, after his expulsion from Allstedt,
told the authorities: 'Stir it up, my dear lords, let the muck give
out a good old stink. I hope you will brew a fine beer out of it,
since you like drinking filth so much', and talked derisively on
one occasion of the 'Wittenberg soup'.[21] A cognate image is that

---

[20]   '*die Grundsuppe*'; WAB 3 Nr. 877, p. 516.
[21]   CW, pp. 114, 157.

Jörg Breu, the Older c. *1530.* 'Smelling the Roast', *Flugblätter, Nr. 7*

of 'smelling the roast', sniffing out trouble, knowing something is 'cooking'.[22]

In his masterly book on the late medieval Church, *The Stripping of the Altars*, Eamonn Duffy celebrates the wealth and vitality of late medieval piety and, by his central metaphor, relates the coming of the Protestant Reformation to the pre-paschal sobriety and desolation of the Tenebrae liturgy, when the church was

---

[22]   In his spirited polemic against Müntzer, the *Letter to the Princes of Saxony* (LW 40, p. 52), Luther talked of the latter 'smelling the roast', to which Müntzer replied: 'I would prefer to smell you roasting in your arrogance in a pot or in a cauldron . . . ' (CW, p. 348).

Crucifix from Utenbach, c. *1500 in* Aller Knecht und Christi Untertan, *p. 357*

stripped of everything colourful and joyous in preparation for the
commemoration of the crucifixion. It has helped to remind us
that the Reformation was quite extraordinarily destructive. The
truth, as Walter Jens has reminded us, often is. Knowledge can be
so brutal that it is identical with annihilation.[23]

I found myself deeply moved by an exhibition in Lutheran
Eisenach in 1996 devoted to iconoclasm. Statues of the saints

---

[23]   '*Die Erkenntnis identisch mit der Vernichtung . . .*'. For the later Alfred
Döblin, now a Christian, truth was more than correctness. It was ruthless,
merciless and filled with religious pathos, not unlike Greek tragedy. Walter
Jens, *Zueignungen. Literarische porträts* (Munich: Piper, 1962), p. 14.

stood there with their eyes gouged out, limbs snapped off, breasts violated. Crucifixes had, as it were, been recrucified. I shuddered and had to wonder at the elemental forces at work here, the power of violence, hate, fear. This, clearly, was a war zone.[24] As Emile Bâle says, it is hard to conceive of the horror of those loyal to the Old Church as they saw scenes such as this.

> In a picture of the Crucifixion Christ had been torn to shreds, while with diabolical irony the figure of the bad thief had been left intact. In a reredos devoted to Saint Michael, the archangel had been destroyed while the demon at his feet was spared.[25]

Now Luther, of course, was no iconoclast, and Calvin never approved of random violence.[26] Iconoclasm in its overt form was but a shadow of the shattering of imaginative categories, the icon within of the myths of continuity, as Luther emphasised, the dreams of harmony and concord. The real idols, as Erhard Schon's 'The Lament of the Images of the Saints' explains, are greed, arrogance and immorality.[27] But even where images of Mary and the saints were not physically removed and the focus was on transforming the image in the heart, 'removing the poison from the snake's fangs', think what it must have meant for contemporaries to engage in dismantling, destruction and demolition on such an unheard-of scale: the destruction of monasteries, for example, and, much more significantly, the subversion of the models of sanctity which they represented, the

---

[24]   *Aller Knecht und Christi Untertan. Der Mensch Luther und sein Unfeld. Katalog der Ausstellungen zum 450. Todesjahr 1996 Wartburg und Eisenach* (Eisenach: Wartburg-Stiftung Eisenach, 1996), pp. 353–60.

[25]   *Religious Art from the Twelfth to the Eighteenth Century* (Princeton: Princeton University Press, 1982), p. 167.

[26]   Ulrich Köpf, 'Die Bilderfrage in der Reformationszeit', *Blätter für Württembergische Kirchengeschichte* 90 (1990), pp. 38–65.

[27]   *Flugblätter der Reformation und des Bauernkrieges* (ed. Hermann Meuche; Leipzig: Insel-Verlag, 1976), Nr. 21.

demolition of much of the Christian year.[28] The dismantling of a whole enchanted world, the disappearance of pilgrimages, relics, indulgences, the hierarchies of angels, many of the great feasts of the Church, the intercession of Mary and the saints.

Our age, combining as it does restless innovation and obsolescence with a growing nostalgia for relics, antiques and memorabilia and a concern for conservation of every kind,[29] may find it hard to grasp, still less approve, this eminently destructive character of the Reformation. It may strike us as uncouth, if not totalitarian, sacrificing the aesthetic to the moralistic. We may dream too easily, perhaps, of a gentler, alternative reform flowing from within, forgetting that, for centuries, reform had been neglected in 'a thousand clerical agendas', as Gordon Rupp put it.[30]

An analogy to the impact of the Reformers may be the challenge of Surrealist art in our century, with its social and political implications and its drive to unmask the banality of the 'beautiful' and release the beauty of the apparently 'banal'. Reformation images often display the same unexpected, disconcerting collocation of images, the tension between 'message' and image, the sense of a *verkehrte Welt*, a world turned upside down. Both in its conception and its reception the Reformation was phenomenally destructive. It was not just the fabric of the buildings or the works of sculptor and artist that were reduced to rubble by iconoclasm, but the loyalties, the networks, the delicate tracery of the spiritual life.

---

[28]   Cf. *Convents Confront the Reformation: Catholic and Protestant Nuns in Germany* (ed. Merry Wiesner-Hanks, tr. Joan Skocir and Merry Wiesner-Hanks; Reformation Texts with Translation: Women of the Reformation, vol. 1; Milwaukee: Marquette University Press, 1996).

[29]   Cf. the remarkable book by David Lowenthal, *The Past is a Foreign Country* (Cambridge: Cambridge University Press, 1985).

[30]   'A Free Church Commemoration', in *London Quarterly and Holborn Review*, 1946, reproduced in *Wisdom and Wit. An Anthology from the Writings of Gordon Rupp* (ed. John A. Vickers; Peterborough: Methodist Publishing House, 1993), p. 108.

Yet, as in Surrealism, such destruction may have been necessary to create *Denkraum*, room to think, space for 'Elijah and Utopia'. It may be that '"Construction" presupposes "Destruction"', as Walter Benjamin has put it.[31] The prevalence of apocalyptic and anticlerical ideas in the late medieval world suggests that for many the intact world, the enchanted universe, was neither intact nor enchanted but shot through with contradictions: the chasm between a remote university theology and lay piety; between the spare *Devotio Moderna* of many reformers, with its ethos of simple discipleship, and the excesses of the popular cult; between the top-heavy institutions of the prelates and the needs of the parish; all the strains and polarities pointed out so long ago by Huizinga.[32] Above all, the tension between an avenging God–Father and a hierarchy of divine intercessors. A vivid depiction of the plague, for example, shows God the Father hurling down his arrows of wrath (subtly bent 'smart weapons') to smite the simple folk, while on the other side Mother Church, the saints, Mary and Christ himself protect the better-off. Schizophrenia appeared to have invaded the divine world itself.[33]

Apocalyptic

Apocalyptic language and thought were not invented by the Reformers. The early sixteenth century was an apocalyptic age, bent under the lash of imminent judgement, convinced that a vast cosmic battle between the forces of good and evil was nearing its climax. Luther's apocalyptic reading of reality was snapped up because it spoke to the deepest intuitions of the age. The dark, whispered memories of the old Hussite traditions, circulating in

---

[31]   *Passagen-Werk* N 7, 6; quoted in Andrew Benjamin and Peter Osborne (eds), *Walter Benjamin's Philosophy. Destruction and Experience* (London and New York: Routledge, 1994), p. x.

[32]   Johan Huizinga, *The Autumn of the Middle Ages* (Chicago: University of Chicago Press, 1996).

[33]   The painting by Martin Schaffner (1477–1547) is dated *c.* 1513; *Reformation in Nürnberg*, p. 184.

oral, written and visual form, talked of the priest–shepherd become a wolf, the vicar–pope an Antichrist. The populist Dominican friar of Florence, Savonarola, the preacher of the despairing at the end of the previous century who predicted imminent plague, invasion and catastrophe because of the sins of Rome, had not been forgotten. The *fin de siècle* pessimism of Sebastian Brant's fabulously successful bestseller, *The Book of Fools*, portrayed life as a dance of death celebrated by fools, each and every reader snap-shotted in woodcut and rhyme as a fool of one kind or another, scholarly, lecherous or whatever, and all embarked on the 'ship of fools' and headed for Narragonia, the land of fools, going nowhere.[34]

In 1476 Hans Beham, the peasant prophet, the Drummer of Niklashausen, was told by the blessed Virgin Mary to gather the true and simple followers of Christ to penitence, for the end was at hand, and to call for the slaughter of the self-serving priests and big shots. Tens of thousands made the pilgrimage to his remote village. *The Nuremberg Chronicle*, written on the cusp of the new century as a universal history and geography of its time, was littered with accounts of monsters and freaks, signs and portents, blood falling from heaven. Albrecht Dürer's *Riders of the Apocalypse* is no doubt the best-known expression of the apprehensions and energy of the age.

In the Reformer Karlstadt's adaptation of Job's term, the whole world resembles an uprooted tree.[35] The art of the period offers us a thousand images of a world split down the middle, individually and corporately.[36] Quite literally, a perpendicular line often ran down the centre of a painting or etching or, less often, laterally across it, with two rival worlds on either side of the line. Such art illustrated the pervasive sense of strain, of rending apart, a great

[34]   Sebastian Brant, *Das Narrenschiff* (ed. H. A. Junghans, and Hans-Joachim Mähl; Stuttgart: Reclam, 1964).
[35]   *The Essential Carlstadt*, p. 31; cf. Job 19.9.
[36]   Cf. Keith Moxey, *Peasants, Warriors and Wives. Popular Imagery in the Reformation* (Chicago and London: University of Chicago Press, 1989).

Unknown artist, c. *1535.* 'World Turned Upside Down!
Hares punish monks and huntsmen', *Flugblätter, Nr. 43*

shattering and shaking of foundations, a world distorted by death
agonies.

Apocalyptic, however, alarming as it might be, was not read in
exclusively negative terms. The death agonies could also be birth
agonies. The prediction that the true and final *haubtenderung,*
cataclysmic change, was at hand gave hope to the depressed and
oppressed, the promise of a breakthrough to a wonderful new era.
Preachers talked of summer being at the door, the harvest being at
hand. The tares would be torn out of the Lord's vineyard. The
elect of the Lord were already, like angels, sharpening their sickles
for the coming harvest, as Thomas Müntzer put it.[37] Artistic
imagination caught mounted armies clashing in the heavens and
blood shafting through the sun, but exuded confidence that the
forces of good would carry off the eventual victory.[38] As contemporary New Testament scholarship reminds us, the temporal

[37]   CW, p. 250.
[38]   As in the woodcut by the 'Meister S.G.', depicting a vision seen in the
skies near Nuremberg in 1554; the stars and the flags borne by the riders were
blue; *Reformation in Nürnberg,* p. 55.

Leonhard Beck. Monk and Donkey, *Flugblätter, Nr. 2, 1523*

reference of apocalyptic to an imminent end can be a way of expressing cultural crisis, political crisis, time as *kairos*, opportunity and openness to the future. For many, apocalyptic was gospel, good news.

Anticlericalism

Anticlericalism, what we might call today a structural critique of the power of the clergy, complemented the urgency of the apocalyptic attitudes to time with new perspectives on the body: the body politic; the body of Christ, the Church; the body of mother earth; all of which had to be reconstituted and resurrected to give the peasant, the artisan, the patrician, the woman, the lay person their rightful place. The 'Petrarca Meister', for example, portrayed the whole of society as a living pillar, rooted on the peasant and culminating in the peasant. This is an astonishing new perspective on rank, place and space.

Mother Church was now perceived by many as 'smothering' Church. There were too many priests and too few of them were

Hans Sebald Behaim. Luxurious Life of Monks, *1521*

educated. What use were they? What was the justification for their exemptions from taxes, civic duties, secular jurisdiction? Friars, monks and upper clergy began to appear as anti-heroes. The true poor were contrasted with the iconised poverty of the monks and the mendicant orders, 'these idle, rich, fat beggars, who ride on great horses . . . who grasp and devour the best houses, fields, grasslands and meadows', as Otto Brunfels put it,[39] but who, as in a dramatic woodcut by Sebald Behaim of Nuremberg, will now be forced to eat their words as the bearer of bad news is literally forced to eat his message. Or is the meaning that they are being forced to digest Scripture? A tattered woman representing poverty confronts the nattily or tartily dressed representations of Avarice, Pride, and *la dolce vita.*[40] German national pride had to be restored. The emperor should no longer kiss the feet of the pope. Clergy should no longer wield the orb

---

[39] *Vom Pfaffenzehnten*, cited by Stayer, *The German Peasants' War . . .* , p. 47.

[40] *Reformation in Nürnberg*, p. 34.

Sale of Indulgences. *Title page of several Augsburg pamphlets, c. 1520*

and the sword.[41] They should no longer be free to prey on people's consciences, entrapping them in their nets.[42]

[41] As in the Nuremberg painter Georg Pencz's 1531 depiction of the subjection of the emperor to the pope; *Reformation in Nürnberg*, p. 42.

[42] *Lazarus Spengler Schriften*, Band 1 (1509–23) (ed. Berndt Hamm and Wolfgang Huber; Quellen und Forschungen zur Reformationsgeschichte, 61; Gütersloh: Gütersloher Verlagshaus, 1995), p. 95/11–15.

Such anticlericalism often stemmed, of course, from indignant clergy themselves. While Doctor Luther stands for *Christum*, not for *Questum* (financial gain), the pope, Karlstadt complained, had become a pickpocket.[43]

Lay people such as Spengler, the city clerk of Nuremberg, waxed equally furious at the commodification of faith, pardons being sold by the indulgence sellers like barrels of pepper at the *jahrmarkt*, the flea-market.[44] The concept of the flea-market is one of most recurrent in the pamphlets of time. The pastor degraded to the level of the huckster.

The tirades against the clergy have, of course, to be taken *cum grano salis*. The accusations of lechery, usury and oppression in a popular song about the Erfurt clergy in 1519 were virtually identical with those hurled against the Jews in Regensburg at the same time. Their synagogue was torn down to make way for the famous shrine to Mary.[45] In both cases the objects of criticism are being scapegoated. People projected on to the clergy their own unresolved personal problems as well as society's structural crises. There is an ugly and ignorant side to much anticlericalism.

The key point about anticlericalism, however, was not its accusations of immorality, ignorance and luxurious living, but its attack on the mediatory role of the priest in penance, the Mass, Extreme Unction, all the sacraments. This not only disempowered the laity, it was perceived as victimising them. Karlstadt declared, in perhaps the most striking of all the polemical metaphors directed against the priesthood, that their very prayers were full of blood. To pay for their services money had been taken from the poor; orphans had died. Instead of giving life, they had taken it away. The contrast with Christ giving his life-blood for the poor was obvious. The point of such criticisms, which can be replicated

[43]   *The Essential Carlstadt*, pp. 49, 94.
[44]   He talks of 'erkaufften selen . . . gleich dem saffran oder pfeffer in pallen und fassen'; *Lazarus Spengler Schriften* 1, 92/7f.
[45]   Freiherr Rochus von Lilliencron (ed.), *Die historischen Volkslieder der Deutschen* (5 vols, Leipzig, 1865–96), 3: pp. 366–9; Nr. 352.

a thousand times, was not that individual clerics had fallen from grace. The whole system was declared corrupt. The new critical historical approach, comparing the current Church with its primitive origins, encouraged the judgement that for four hundred years (or was it a thousand years?) the Church itself had fallen from its divine vocation.

Such pronouncements pulled the linchpin out of a whole spiritual universe. The spell of the enchanted universe was shattered, the symbolic power of the priest challenged. This far transcended a mere moral or social critique. Salvation and liberation were at stake. Apocalyptic expectations had combined with a fierce anticlerical critique to stir the pot furiously. People were already beginning to 'smell the roast'.[46]

[46] A fine broadsheet treatment of this topic can be found in Der Bratenriecher, c. 1535; *Flugblätter der Reformation*, Nr. 7; cf. p. 12 above.

CHAPTER TWO

A NEW SONG OR
THE STRIPPING OF THE ALTARS?

On the coasts of New Zealand the surf meets the shore in serried ranks of breakers, often as much as seven lines of waves one behind another. The waves of sermons, songs, poems, pamphlets, broadsheets and books which heralded the Reformation message remind me of that in their quiet relentlessness. On the other hand, sometimes as you approach the beach, hidden behind high sand dunes, you suddenly catch sight of the great arc of the bay and, as the thunder of the surf fills your ears and the spray hangs in the air, you know you are in the presence of something quite awesome. The same is true of the Reformation.

In this chapter we shall examine some of the primary, primal images which captured mind and heart. We shall argue that poet, artist, musician, printer and pamphleteer allied with preacher so that, in Luther's words, the Gospel was not only preached, but painted, sung, and – we might add – rhymed: *gepredigt, gemalt, geschrieben und gesungen.*[1] Thomas Müntzer and the shoemaker

---

[1] Cf. *Wider die himmlischen Propheten*, W 18, pp. 37–125. On this area cf. Max Geisberg, *The German Single-Leaf Woodcut: 1500–1550* (New York: Hacker Art Book, 1974); this contains innumerable images of Scripture, anticlericalism, apocalyptic themes, peasant life, women, justice and injustice; Fritz Saxl, *Lectures*, vol. I (London: Warburg Institute, 1957); Konrad Hoffman, 'Typologie, Exemplarik und reformatorische Bildsatire', in *Kontinuität und Umbruch: Theologie und Froemmigkeit in Flugschriften und Kleinliteratur an der Wende vom 15. zum 16 Jahrhundert* (Stuttgart: Klett-Cotta, 1978); Richard Cole, 'Pamphlet Woodcuts in the Communication Process of Reformation Germany', in *Pietas et Societas. New Trends in Reformation Social History* (ed.

Hans Sachs talked similarly of preaching, printing, and singing.[2] The Reformation, this chapter will argue, was more a song or a symphony than a system, more lyric than lecture, more a leap of the imagination than one of those social restructurings we are so heartily sick of today. It certainly produced systems, lectures and structures as well, but they were secondary.

The vernacular liturgy which Thomas Müntzer pioneered for the people of the little town of Allstedt in 1523 was for him the new song of the Spirit. It enabled people to 'sing along'; the old Gregorian chants were retained, but now as participatory, not choral, worship. 'Through the singing of simple and familiar tunes the unlettered would become more receptive to God's Spirit than through formal study of the Scriptures.'[3] For Müntzer, as for all the Reformers, the Psalms, the key of David, opened the door to all true worship. Christ bears the key of David on his shoulder.[4] For Müntzer printing was another eschatological tool, God-given to gather the elect and reach a universal audience. To all intents and purposes it was a trumpet fanfare. The truth of God was often conceived as a trumpet blast. The trumpets of the Word of God, as Luther depicted it unforgettably in his *Appeal to the German Nobility*, would shatter the walls of Jericho, the defensive ramparts of clerical self-interest.

The pamphlets of this period, therefore, should not be seen in anachronistic terms as propaganda but – to amend Clausewitz's dictum – as an extension of preaching and pastoring by other means, a yell of protest, a cry of adoration. Printing had the further advantage of being easier of access for the non-ordained, even women. The lively and relatively expensive woodcuts on the front

---

Kyle C. Sessions and Philip N. Bebb; Kirksville, MO, 1985), pp. 103–21; Rainer Wohlfeil, 'Lutherische Bildtheologie', *Martin Luther Probleme seiner Zeit* (ed. Volker Press and Dieter Stievermann; Stuttgart, 1986), pp. 282–93.

    [2]   CW, p. 68.

    [3]   Tom Scott, *Thomas Müntzer. Theology and Revolution in the German Reformation* (London: Macmillan, 1989), p. 51.

    [4]   CW, p. 170.

promised diversion, 'infotainment', as well as revelation. And one could now buy a New Testament for the cost of a couple of rabbits for the stew. Printers, who were often enthusiastic supporters of the reform movement, were in some ways the new priests, the 'connection people' who complemented the work of the preachers.[5] The printing press, to use Walter Wink's modern terminology, enabled people to name, to unmask and to engage 'the beast'.[6] The language of 'unmasking' is frequently used in the pamphlets themselves, to underline the quest for openness and authenticity.

Preaching, to an extent unimaginable today, was also a public act, where realities could be placarded for all to hear, programmes outlined, opponents 'named'. The enthusiasm for sermons is well documented. Clearly something very different from the traditional moral homilies or revivalist harangues was being offered. As we shall see, it was, at its best, not didactic but kerygmatic, pointing to Christ.

The 'new song' of the Reformation celebrated an age of new frontiers when the old symbolic markers were collapsing. Visually and verbally, pamphlets portrayed the discoveries of the New World. But quite apart from this awareness that, literally and geographically, the world was expanding, there was a growing sense that the old ways would no longer do. Culturally, humanism broke down one barrier after another. What a wonderful time to be living in, Hutten and a whole army of young humanists cried, hailing the rediscovery of the ancient glories of Greece and Rome – yes, and of apostolic Christianity too; whole constellations of scholarship becoming available in new editions, the languages emerged from centuries of barbarism; a learned piety and social harmony were pursued not only for their sensitivity to civilised values, precious as that was, but because they reflected God's good will in creation, the divine image in humanity. Law, diplomacy

[5]   Russell Hoban, *Riddley Walker* (London: Pan, 1992).
[6]   Walter Wink, *Engaging the Powers: Discernment and Resistance in a World of Domination* (Minnesota: Fortress Press, 1992).

and education were all being renewed. More's Utopia. A new humanity in birth!

The new vogue for dialogue, satire and narrative history gave priority to story-telling, to the *via rhetorica* over the *via dialectica*; conversation, intuition and empathetic imagination took over from logic, paradox from syllogism, open disputations in the 'public square' from magisterial pronouncements behind closed doors. These are not just matters of style and form. They point to a fundamentally new way of perceiving and presenting the truth.

Luther's popularity was as 'Dr Luther'. He represented to an impatient generation the impossible possibility of an intelligent theologian, one who was a champion of Scripture and the languages, the giant-killer of Aristotle. As a furious Hugo Marschalck put it in his racy defence of 'our Luther', his name meant *lauter*, pure, not *lotter*, corrupt. To have been grotesquely attacked by those unlearned tyrants who claimed the name of the gentle Christ but worshipped their idol the pope was to his credit.[7] For lay people Luther was the still more impossible possibility of a 'with it' theologian, a scholar who knew the language of the street and met an epidemic of ignorance with a medicine accessible to all.[8] For Luther, human speech itself was a sacrament.

So let us attempt to engage with this sacramental world of language, enter this ocean of metaphors. A host of new images sought to catch the mood, the tonality of the age. Pamphlets, sermons, woodcuts and paintings referred continually to waking up, to the dawning of a new age, to light replacing darkness, to freedom overthrowing tyranny. There is repeated reference to the living Word of God, in itself an extraordinary image when one thinks about it, and among the biblical images those of deliverance are perhaps the most prominent: Moses and Egypt,

---

[7]   *Von dem weyt erschollen Namen Luthers* . . . (Strasburg, 1523), Fiche 10/41.

[8]   *Lazarus Spengler Schriften*, 1, pp. 98f.

Deborah, Daniel and the lion's den, the ever-present resurrection lamb.[9]

In its iconic creativity the Reformation had at least one immediate predecessor: the Hussite revolution.[10] John Huss became St John Huss and began to replace the traditional saints in the popular Bohemian tradition. He was their man, burnt to death on an aching stake in Constance in 1415, but only now truly alive; the resurrection motif is powerfully present. The mocking paper crown put on his head as he was led off to be burnt alive became a crown of honour, a hall-mark of discipleship, the symbol of a Church in which lay people stood tall, and Christ was all in all.[11]

Huss was celebrated as much in song as in manifesto, in symbolic representations in books or on flags as much as in resolutions. In the Utraquist and Taborite world of his followers, the visual depiction of the chalice, demonstrating that Christ was accessible to all, not just the clergy, was to be seen everywhere, together with that of the vernacular Bible. This was complemented by a slashing attack on adoration of the saints, the papacy and the mediatorial role of the priesthood.

The continuing vibrancy of this oral tradition of John Huss, martyred almost exactly a century before, is very striking: his emphasis on the law of God, God exegeting the text of reality in one's own tongue, is celebrated in countless tracts, woodcuts and

[9]   There was, of course, also a host of negative imagery, verbal and visual. The pope was likened to a grotesque monster, found in the River Tiber, near Rome; or seen as Antichrist, the living incarnation of the Devil; such bizarre and obscene images of disgust and hate could draw on a long tradition of humanist and popular satire. Cf. Matheson, *The Rhetoric of the Reformation*, esp. the chapter on 'The Down-side of Polemic', pp. 183–214.

[10]   Thomas A. Fudge, '"The Crown" and the "Red Gown": Hussite Popular Religion', in Bob Scribner and Trevor Johnson (eds), *Popular Religion in Germany and Central Europe. 1400–1800* (London: Macmillan, 1996), pp. 38–57.

[11]   It is interesting that Karl Barth reminded us of Huss in the dark days of 1938.

paintings. The sermon by Bugenhagen at Luther's funeral recalled Huss's prediction that though he was to be roasted as a goose (= *Huss* in Bohemian), God would raise up a swan in his place, a prediction fulfilled in Luther.[12] The attack on Luther as a Hussite, most famously by John Eck in 1519, proved dramatically counter-productive. The Reformation stood in a proud revolutionary tradition.[13]

As we move to the sixteenth-century Reformation we are immediately struck by the same coinherence of the verbal, the visual and the musical that we have seen in the Hussite movement. Luther is represented as a lute player and as a nightingale.[14] The call for a decisive break with the papacy was represented in woodcut after woodcut, painting after painting, by a division running right down the centre of the picture or between top and bottom. This represents the 'terrible shattering', which ran through individuals as well as communities torn between in-eluctable choices, agonising tugs of loyalty, between beginnings and endings. A famous painting of Cranach, for example, *An Allegory of Grace and Law*, equates the choice for or against the Reformation with choosing between heaven and hell, Christ and Moses, life and death. Christ is the victorious Easter Lamb. He

---

[12]   *Eine Christliche Predigt/ vber der Leich vnd begrebnis/des Ehrwirdigen D. Martini Luthers* . . . B i in *Vom Christlichen abschied aus diesem tödlichen leben des Ehrwirdigen Herrn D. Martini Lutheri. Drei zeitgenössische Texte zum Tode D. Martin Luthers*. Mit einer Einführung von Peter Freybe . . . und einem Nachwort . . . von Siegfried Bräuer (Stuttgart: Verlag Joachim W. Siener, 1996).

[13]   The two-volume history of Huss by Mattheus Flacius Illyricus, *Ioannis Hus et Hieronymi Pragensis confessorum Christi historia*, published in Nuremberg in 1558, has recently been shown to be the inspiration for John Foxe's icon-ography of Huss: Mary Aston and Elizabeth Ingram, 'The Iconography of the Acts and Monuments', in *John Foxe and the English Reformation* (ed. David Loades; Aldershot: Scolar Press, 1997), pp. 66–142.

[14]   In C. J. Visscher's (*c.* 1570) invocation of religious tolerance in which all, including the pope, Luther, Calvin and the Anabaptists, prepare their own meal in a great kitchen, Luther is seen playing the lute. Cf. Salvatore Caponetto, *La Riforma protestante nell'Italia del Cinquecento* (2nd edition, Turin, 1997), p. 109.

Lucas Cranach. Law and Gospel, *1529*

treads down death and the dragon. There even seems to be an ecological touch, with a green fertile world contrasted with a universe that seems to be blighted with acid rain.[15]

A woodcut by the 'Petrarca Meister' portrays on the left a new age opening up, as the cock crows to hail the dawn; on the right the hail of present vicissitudes continues to rain down, devastating crops and alarming a cowering walker.[16] The poem by Hans Sachs in 1523, with its famous woodcut representing Luther as the nightingale which, of course, sings while it is still night, emphasised that his song was now being heard everywhere. Luke 19 is placarded: if these were silent the very stones would cry out! As the nightingale sings, the sheep gather around the tree, which divides off day from night. In the background the emblematic lamb of God is triumphant while Luther's Old Church opponents, bestialised as cats or goats, cluster in frustrated rage around the

[15] *Allegorie auf Gesetz und Gnade.* After 1529.
[16] Maurice Pianzola, *Bauern und Künstler. Die Künstler der Renaissance und der Bauernkrieg von 1525* (tr. Tilly Bergner; Berlin: Henschelverlag, 1961), p. 67.

Petrarca Meister. The Expectation of a Better Time, *1519/20*

tree.[17] Luther is a herald, an angel, a prophet, pointing to the light of Christ.[18] He has become an icon himself, a saint.[19]

Another very pervasive image of the Reformation period, going back to Erasmus himself,[20] was that of leaving the muddy lagoon of a corrupt tradition for the pure sources of truth. Truth, for

---

[17]   Hans Sachs, *Die Wittenbergisch Nachtigall* (ed. Gerald H. Seufert; Stuttgart: Reclam, 1974).

[18]   The impact can be heightened by the deconstruction of old loyalties. A peasant in a pamphlet dialogue, for example, is told by St Peter that Luther is his true follower, not the pope. Chrisman, *Conflicting Visions*, 120. 4.

[19]   On the development of this concept, cf. Bob Scribner, *Popular Culture and Popular Movements in Reformation Germany* (London: Hambledon Press, 1987), esp. chs 14 and 15.

[20]   And no doubt to biblical images from Jeremiah, Ezekiel and elsewhere, behind that. I am grateful to Professor Graeme Auld for pointing this out. A favourite text for Argula von Grumbach, for example, is Jeremiah 2.13, forsaking the well of living water for broken cisterns. *Argula von Grumbach. A Woman's Voice in the Reformation* (ed. and tr. Peter Matheson; Edinburgh: T. & T. Clark, 1995), pp. 90, 188.

Die Wittenbergisch Nachtigall
Die man yetz höret überall.

Ich sage euch/wa dise schweygē/so werdē die stayn schreyen Luce 19.

Title page of Hans Sachs, Die Wittenbergisch Nachtigall, *Nüremberg, 1523*

the humanist, lay at the beginning of things. We have to get back to the sources, *ad fontes,* the original classics; in the case of Christianity, the prophets, the evangelists and the apostles. In the place of idolatrous mud-puddles, as Karlstadt put it, people needed, and were now getting access to, the pure streams

Hans Holbein, the Younger. Luther as the German Hercules, 1528

of truth.[21] Others talked of the flowing, curative waters of Wittenberg; or of regaining the juice of Holy Scripture of which the papists had robbed us.[22] The way forward is back!

[21]   *The Essential Carlstadt*, p. 262.
[22]   *safft; Lazarus Spengler Schriften* 1, p. 87/4.

Woodcut from Thomas Murner's The Great Lutheran Fool, *1522,*
accusing Luther of stealing flag of freedom

In Charles Frazier's remarkable first novel, *Cold Mountain*,
Inman, returning from the hideousness of the Civil War in the
US, looks at a mountain stream and reflects that whatever moves
has to adapt itself to the maze that is the actual landscape in which

it finds itself.[23] A purist, essentialist reading of the Reformation is blind to all that. Subjectively, however, that was the intention of the Reformers: to live by the crystal pure waters and nothing else.

Images of the new dawn, of awaking from slumber, of returning to the sources of pure water jostle together with images of freedom.[24] Freedom, of course, is an expansive concept, into which people feed their own expectations. One of the advances in recent scholarship is the attention given by scholars such as Miriam Chrisman and Lorna Abray to the great variety of lay visions of reform. Freedom was a central motif, but the understanding of freedom depended largely on where one came in society.[25] The imperial knights thought of their traditional liberties. Artisans yearned for free access to Scripture. Lazarus Spengler, the city clerk of Nuremberg, declared: 'Everything to do with the Gospel, faith, and the Christian life should be utterly free.'[26] Freedom from fear, ceremonies and canon law; freedom from the devil's dungeon of compulsory celibacy, as Karlstadt put it.[27] Tyranny, likewise, was very differently perceived. When the revolutionary peasants waved their flag, with its symbol of the *Bundschuh*, the peasant's boot, they understood freedom to mean liberation from serfdom. These flags brought heaven down to earth. They were also a vehement protest against the use of the cross on the flags or armour of princely armies, which was an insufferable insult to 'our beloved Christ', the champion of

---

[23]   Charles Frazier, *Cold Mountain* (New York: Grove-Atlantic, 1997).

[24]   One of the most striking images is that of a woodcut, from *c.* 1520, which depicts a rebellious peasant striding from left to right, a sword horizontal across his body, holding a billowing flag inscribed with one word: *frÿheit*.

[25]   Chrisman, *Conflicting Visions*, passim; Lorna Jane Abray, *The People's Reformation. Magistrates, Clergy, and Commons in Strasbourg, 1500–1598* (Oxford: Basil Blackwell, 1985).

[26]   *Dann alles, das evangelisch, christlich oder im glauben ist, das sol gantz frey sein . . . Lazarus Spengler Schriften* 1, pp. 287/7f.

[27]   *The Essential Carlstadt*, p. 130.

Lucas Cranach, the Older. Luther as Preacher, *1548*

peace and reconciliation.[28] Poignantly, the peasants at the battle of Frankenhausen in 1525, which ended in a dreadful massacre, saw their rainbow flag mirrored in the 'rainbow' in the sky above them, a halo around the sun, just before the battle began, and took it to be a sign of God's favour.

Another concern was freedom for the truth. The truth, the humanist Reuchlin had declared, is invincible or, as Hubmaier put it, immortal. A thousand sermons talk of the chained, corrupted Gospel being set free. Luther's supreme achievement was seen as letting the Word run free. The famous Cranach painting sums it all up: Luther, on the right, preaches from the open Bible, facing the congregation on the left but pointing to the crucified Christ in the centre. This speaks a thousand times more eloquently than a hundred disquisitions on the theology of the Word, of a different understanding of church, worship, language. Perhaps the most pervasive image of the Reformation is that of the liberated Word of God.

Much of this iconography of freedom, of course, remained aspiration, not reality. The peasants at Frankenhausen perished miserably. Whether or not freedom became a reality, it had captured the high ground of the imagination. The old enchanted world was relegated because for many it had become an accursed world, a tyranny, and a more liberating one had replaced it.

As the continuum of tradition and authority, male tradition and clerical authority, was challenged, concepts of time began to shift. The key issues in the early Reformation – the pure Gospel and lay participation in the life and thinking of the Church – relativised both the authority of the clerical élite and canonical traditions. This facilitated a recovery of eschatological brokenness and openness to the *kairos*, the presence of the now.

A new grid was put upon space, too. The understanding of a holy place was radically challenged, as humanism had already done

[28]   Johannes Locher, *Ein ungewöhnlicher zweiter Sendbrief des Bauernfeinds an Karsthans, in Flugschriften der Bauernkriegszeit* (ed. Adolf Laube, etc.; Berlin: Akademie-Verlag, 1975), p. 101/4–9.

to some extent. The availability of the printed book and pamphlet allowed the private scrutiny of public verities. On the other hand, the discussion of Scripture and theology moved from behind the closed doors and privileged space of academy and church into public space. Part of the offensiveness of Argula von Grumbach, the woman Reformer of Bavaria, is that she left her proper domestic space as a woman and claimed access to public space for herself and her ideas. A woodcut depicted Argula von Grumbach, mother of four, Bible in hand, confronting a whole team of bemused theologians. Lying discarded on the ground are the tomes of canon law. Her confident, 'free' body language says it all.[29] The debate between Argula and the Ingolstadt theologians never took place. But in the imagination of her readers it should have, and in the form of her pamphlets it did.

Walter Benjamin, writing in the early 1930s when the horrors of the Third Reich still seemed attractive to most right-thinking, *Daily Telegraph* reading people, talked of the need for a new landscape, 'the contours that the telescope will show in a future world freed from magic'.[30] His Marxist and Jewish perspectives may help us to grasp what a remarkable and all-encompassing revolution the Reformation was. It offered a new landscape.[31] Not freedom of speech in the modern, secularised sense of an individual's right to hear and be heard, but in the sense of a limitation on all institutional hindrances to the freedom of the Word.

[29]   Matthes Maler's Erfurt edition of her letter to the University of Ingolstadt of 1523 uses this woodcut as its frontispiece.

[30]   *Benjamin*, p. 206.

[31]   An interesting recent treatment of 'freedom' in the German-speaking Reformation by Peter Blickle suggests that it was understood in a republican, communal sense rather than in the individualist, private property-centred way of the Anglo-Saxon world. 'Reformation und Freiheit', *Die frühe Reformation in Deutschland als Umbruch. Wissenschaftliches Symposion des Vereins für Reformationsgeschichte 1996* (Schriften des Vereins fur Reformationsgeschichte Nr. 199; ed. Bernd Moeller, with Stephen E. Buckwalter; Gütersloh: Gütersloher Verlagshaus, 1998).

Another favourite image of the Reformers, as it was, of course, of the eighteenth-century Enlightenment, was the biblical metaphor of light. It is prominent in one of most popular hymns in the sixteenth century: Lazarus Spengler's hymn of 1524, 'Durch Adams Fall'. Spengler was one of many lay people who were moved to write poetry, songs and hymns.

> Meyn fussen ist deyn heyliges wort
> eyn brynnende lucern
> eyn liecht, das myr den weg weyst fort;
> so diser Morgenstern
> yn uns auffgeht.

> A flaming lantern to my feet
> Your holy word
> A light to show the way ahead
> A shining morning star
> Within our hearts.[32]

Sermons, pamphlets and woodcuts emphasised the need to get things out into the light. The light of the Gospel has been revealed again to this generation, so we have a peculiar responsibility to let it shine out. Christian truth should be open and accessible to all – like a candle on a candlestick, in *publico und nit in den schulen*, in public and not confined to the universities.[33] Hans Sachs satirised those who, like the owl, shun the light of day (the owl was as often a symbol of stubborn sinfulness as of wisdom) and, despite all the aids to vision – the sun, a candle, spectacles – refuse to come into the light. We should wake up and repent, for Christ is the sun of righteousness.[34]

---

[32]   *Lazarus Spengler Schriften* 1, p. 404; Thomas Stör uses identical imagery: John the Baptist is a flaming lantern, *'ein brinnende lucern'*; Christ's followers are to be *brinnende aufgestackte liechter lebendiger Exempel*, 'erect, flaming lights of living examples' (Matthew 5.14ff.); he talks of the 'joyous morning star of the divine word'; *Von dem Christlichen Weingarten . . .* Aiv; Hiii; Fiche 92/261.

[33]   Ibid., 99/19.

[34]   *Was hilft mich sun liecht oder prill/ wyl ich doch selbs nicht sehen will. Flugblätter der Reformation*, Nr. 22.

Erhard Schön. Owl Shuns the Light, c. *1540, Flugblätter, Nr. 22*

This concern for light, transparency, access to the truth, appears to have been a particular concern of lay men and women such as Argula von Grumbach. We have the light, so why hide it? 'It is my heartfelt wish that this light should dwell in all of us and shine upon all callous and blinded hearts.'[35] God is light and we have the duty (and the joy – light is almost always associated with joy) to broadcast this light. The transfiguration became a symbol for the life of all true Christians; as Thomas Müntzer put it, their whole inward being was to be flooded, suffused with light.[36]

Any scholarly, clerical exclusiveness which hoarded the truth, clutched it to itself, restricted discussion to a particular caste, venue, profession or élite was to be resisted. The public arena was

---

[35] AvG, p. 75.
[36] The outward pretence of piety was replaced by the *'erglastung Gotis im liecht zum liechte'*. MSB 2223/15.

sought, and 'hole and corner' processes deplored. The truth was to be trumpeted forth, placarded in large letters to the world. A favourite image of Thomas Müntzer, taken from the domestic chest in which valuables were stored, was to 'take the lid off', to bring things out into the open, into the light, to 'be quite frank about the truth of the Bible before the whole world'.[37] Under persecution a key strategy for Christians was to use the printing press to expose the faults of the powerful so that everyone scorned them. 'So if it does appear in print for the whole world to see, then you can count on the understanding of all Christian people.'[38]

None of this was easy, either for individuals or communities. Hope ground against despair, anticipation against world-weariness, and new depths of pain and doubt had to be plumbed in the quest for answers. Luther himself, of course, talked famously of *Anfechtung*, an athletic wrestling not unlike that of Jacob on the Jabbok, a writhing on the cross of reality. Others used the more mystical images of the dark night of the soul: darkness, purgation, sinking to the bottom of a river, the acceptance of suffering, *resignatio, gelassenheit*.

In all this, the centrality of Scripture is evident, but we may have to revisit our understanding of the way in which Scripture came alive. The Reformers did not dredge Scripture for proof-texts. The Bible's light and clarity were not so much a doctrinal source or a blueprint for structural change. Rather, when we read their sermons and pamphlets we find biblical personalities and images swimming up to the surface of their minds. An irruption, explosion, eruption of the biblical imagination of the patriarchs, prophets, psalmists and apostles took place.[39]

---

[37]   CW, p. 68.

[38]   CW, p. 133.

[39]   One is reminded of the connections traced by the contemporary biblical scholar Walter Brueggemann between images rising out of the unconscious and the way in which scriptural texts impinge on us: *Texts Under Negotiation. The Bible and Postmodern Imagination* (Minneapolis: Fortress Press, 1993), esp. pp. 21–5.

Certainly Huldah, Gideon, Elijah, Daniel, John the Baptist, Mary Magdalene and the apostle Paul leapt to life in contemporary form. In one sense there was nothing new about this. No one who has seen medieval tapestry or stained glass windows can ever forget how the biblical figures have always been actualised, so that they walked the stage in contemporary costume and posture.[40] But John Colet, Jacques Lefevre and Erasmus himself had pioneered a new hermeneutic, warmly adapted by the Reformers, in which they learnt to sink themselves, heart and mind, into the tonality of the biblical world. They thought deeply about the way in which biblical concerns had to be accommodated to radically different situations. As Packull points out, 'hermeneutic communities' were formed by the Anabaptists, who equipped their lay members with tools to find their way around Scripture. 'A situational reading of the Scriptures predisposed readers towards specific biblical texts or stories and influenced interpretation.'[41]

Much attention has rightly been paid to the importance of the vernacular language of Reformation hymns and psalms. But allowing people to read in their own distinctive dialect is only part of this wider recovery of the earthy humanity of Scripture. Colet came to see that Paul's writings were not proof-texts, cannon-fodder for doctrinal verities arrived at elsewhere (to venture a gruesome pun), but letters addressed at a particular time to meet situations in a particular place. The dramatic dimensions to the Gospels were discovered, and the songs of Deborah and Mary's Magnificat were rediscovered as the lyrics of the oppressed. The prophets were read politically and not just spiritually. All this surfaced in the popular imagination with unbelievable éclat. Gerard Roussel, reporting on the singing of the psalms in Strasburg, talked of them 'ravishing the soul'.[42] The God-givenness

[40]   Cf. Emile Bâle, *Religious Art*, pp. 124f.

[41]   Werner O. Packull, *Hutterite Beginnings: Communitarian experiments during the Reformation* (Baltimore and London: Johns Hopkins University Press, 1995), pp. 17f.

[42]   Herminjard 1 Nr. 167 to Bishop of Meaux, Dec. 1525, p. 408.

of Scripture was recognised precisely because it resonated in the depths of people's experience.

This leads us to the epicentre of the Reformers' proclamation, that God is supremely revealed in the lowly figure of Christ. But again we should not assume that an academic approach to this, by way of christological reflection, is necessarily the best gateway to see how they understood Christ. When studying the way in which Argula von Grumbach or Müntzer used Scripture, I have been struck by the clustering of the texts around particular images of saltiness, for example, or of light.[43] The Franciscan Benedetto Locarno, preaching in Bologna in 1543, likened justification by faith to the waves of a great sea, the ocean which is Christ, whose saltiness becomes our wisdom and righteousness.[44]

Hence it may be helpful to think of each of the Reformers as having a personalised canon in their head which linked together texts from Psalms and Paul, Numbers and Revelation. Luther's breakthrough to a new understanding of righteousness is described in this way. But it is true of lay people as well. Argula von Grumbach, for example, talks of flitting from text to text, leaping, as it were, from one stepping stone to the next. 'Ah, but what a joy it is when the spirit of God teaches us and gives us understanding, flitting from one text to the next . . .'[45] The process is less a strictly logical one than an associative one which sets up a chain of images. We may have to ask of each of the Reformers, and of all their listeners: What was the controlling image of their sermons, songs or writings? How did they think of Christ as that 'master-image'?

It is intriguing to see how lay people interpreted the centrality of Christ. Count Albrecht of Mansfeld wrote a letter in January 1525 to his relatives in defence of his wife's receiving the Lord's Supper in both kinds. Christ is mentioned more than twenty

---

[43]   Peter Matheson, 'Whose Scripture? A Venture into Reformation Hermeneutics', *The Mennonite Quarterly Review* LXX (April 1996), pp. 191–202.

[44]   The image of the sea is taken from Cusanus; cf. Caponetto, pp. 32, 483.

[45]   AvG, p. 86.

times, almost always in connection with his institution of the sacraments. Christ our saviour, Albrecht says, is no cobbler or tailor's apprentice but the highest and only head of Christendom, '*das oberste vnnd einiche heubt der christenheit*'. Christ is the supreme emperor, whose word is the only one that counts, a word unanimously witnessed to by four evangelists, brim-full of the Holy Spirit, charged with wisdom and power, not by drunken, brainless idiots. It is not to be confused with Luther's, either!

For this evangelical prince who already sees himself as a Protestant, although the emergence of Protestantism is usually dated after the Diet of Speyer in 1529, God's holy Word is imaged not as a book but as the princely Christ, a legislator who speaks '*gewyß, clar vnnd war*', authoritatively, clearly, truly, and whose institution of the Lord's Supper has to be followed '*gantz vnnd frey*', unflinchingly, without qualification.[46]

Another layman, Lazarus Spengler, focuses more typically, no doubt, on the cross of Christ. The best medicine for us is adversity, the cross of daily *Anfechtung*, where we encounter Christ as our one redeemer and saviour, following him and being conformed to him in his suffering and sadness. We see here the influence of Staupitz and the late mystical contemplation of the wounds of Christ, as mediated through Luther. Christ's elevation is not in the Mass but, like the serpent in the wilderness, Christ is a sign, a promise for us, a metaphor of our spiritual health and eternal salvation. We are to 'cling to Christ', to his merit, efforts, grace and mercy, and not to our works; dipping the garment of our good works in the blood of Christ to be washed clean.[47] Calvin

---

[46]   Haupstaatsarchiv Weimar, Reg. Ee. 370. Bl. 1ʳ-11ᵛ; transcribed by Siegfried Bräuer, 'Luthers "Zwei-Reiche-Lehre" im Ernstfall. Der Konflikt Graf Albrechts von Mansfeld mit seinen Vettern wegen reformatorischer Neuerungen 1524/25' in *Landesgeschichte als Herausforderung und Programm. Karlheinz Blaschke zum 70. Geburtstag* (ed. Uwe John and Josef Matzerath; Stuttgart: Verlag der Sächsischen Akademie der Wissenschaften zu Leipzig, 1998), pp. 299–304; cf. the reference to the *protestacion* of the evangelical estates at the Nuremberg Diet of 1524, 301f.

[47]   *Lazarus Spengler Schriften* 1, pp. 420/5ff., 426/11f., 91/9ff.

too, of course, made much of the Pauline image of putting off the old and putting on the new humanity, renewed in the image of God. There are many variants on this image.

The artisan or peasant view emphasises the humanity and poverty of Jesus, who suffered hunger and cold like them, and also the temptations of the devil. 'Comforting and sweet Jesus Christ, our redeemer and creator, our brother in genuine flesh and blood. Ah, dear lord, make us good, too.'[48] The bloody sweat of Christ is often closely related to the blood and sweat of the labourer. By Christ's precious blood we, too, have been set free, as the articles of the peasants have it, rejecting serfdom.[49] The crucified Lord is almost always accompanied, in the iconography of the time, by the resurrection lamb. Note, though, that even the symbol of God's triumph is a gentle one.

We will close this chapter with one of Luther's most memorable images, that of the wall, or rather the storming of walls. The *Appeal to the German Nobility* of 1520, next to his Bible perhaps his most influential writing, begins with the famous visualisation of the three walls of immunities with which the Romanists, as he called them, had protected themselves. They had built a city of privilege, whose defensive ramparts were their spiritual superiority to lay people, their authority over Scripture and church councils. But, as in ancient Jericho, they will come tumbling down when the war trumpets are sounded, the clarion call for God's justice and truth. The city of God is no privileged place, but accessible to all with faith.

The wall, the defensive rampart, a familiar sight around every market town, can also be used positively in Reformation imagery. Probably Luther's best known hymn in the Anglo-Saxon world, 'Ein feste Burg' presents God as a firm fortress, impregnable against all assaults of the Devil. Faith, says Karlstadt, in a rather

[48]   Niklaus Manuel, *Ein Fassnacht spyl*. Fiche 938/2345.
[49]   Cf. the Memmingen articles of March 1525, Nr. 3: *The German Peasants' War. A History in Documents* (ed. and tr. Tom Scott and Bob Scribner; New Jersey; Humanities Press, 1991), p. 78.

lovely biblical metaphor, is a *hortus inclusus*,[50] an enclosed garden, walled-in and protected by Scripture. Sometimes the Reformers also adopted the image of the iron wall in Jeremiah 1, shielding the house of God from the attacks of the ungodly, as an emblem of their staunchness or prophetic zeal.[51]

Freedom, light, the new dawn, waking from slumber, the eternal league or covenant, Zion itself, the holy city, Christ on the cross, the resurrection lamb, the key of the knowledge of God, the new apostolic church – the list of images is endless. This chapter cannot give anything like an exhaustive listing even of the most prominent ones. It rather illustrates a thesis, that it was by such primal, powerful and overwhelmingly biblical images that the Reformation found a purchase on people's minds and hearts. In printing, preaching, song and art the voiceless were given a voice, the visionless a vision. Yet this could not be called a populist gospel any more than it was a biblicist one. The Christ of the poor who emerged was also the Christ of the gospels. The marginalised of the sixteenth century woke to find themselves central to the message of the prophets, the apostles and Jesus. Scripture was not a window to a distant historical past, nor a mere mirror of their own aspirations. The living Word of God spoke to their dangerous memories precisely because it was earthed in a soil so similar to theirs.[52]

---

[50] *The Essential Carlstadt*, p. 32; or a kernel in a nut, ibid., p. 203.

[51] Martin Bucer told Philip of Hesse at the end of November 1541 that we Protestants (*Protestierenden*) have to stand firm against Romanist attacks. Max Lenz, *Briefwechsel Landgraf Phillipps' des Grossmütigen von Hessen mit Bucer* (Leipzig, 1880–91), vol. 2, Nr. 129, p. 31; Thomas Müntzer frequently used the image of being a defensive wall.

[52] Caution may be in place, however, about arguing that this use of images was a conscious process by which the élite in society created a new identity: 'The Protestant writers employed images and metaphors in their writings which were taken from scripture and intended to shape the minds of men and women, and to influence their perceptions and ways of acting.' *Protestant History and Identity in Sixteenth-Century Europe*, vol. 2, *The Later Reformation* (ed. Bruce Gordon; Aldershot: Scolar Press, 1996), p. 22.

In the next chapter we shall focus specifically on the images of justice, harmony and peace embodied in the communal dreams of country people and city dwellers as, with extraordinary hope and determination, the Reformers sought to incarnate the Utopian dreams of humanist and humble folk alike in village and urban life.

CHAPTER THREE

RURAL AND URBAN UTOPIAS

The early sixteenth century was eminently Utopian. We think immediately of Thomas More's *Utopia*, or the *Wolfaria* of Eberlin von Günzburg, Martin Bucer's *Kingdom of Christ*, Campanella's *City of the Sun*; but equally important were the endeavours of countless humanists and imperial knights, villagers and artisans, magisterial reformers and Anabaptists to recast the whole face of reality so that our 'earthly life may soar up to heaven'.[1] There was a wide and deep apprehension that the times were out of joint. Humanism, Catholic reformism, German nationalism, mystical, evangelical and apocalyptic movements all contributed their stalks to the sheaf of discontent. More importantly, they offered exciting alternative visions for church and state, classical and biblical blueprints which focused the yearning for a new ordering of things, a recovery of the divine *ordo rerum*. A mark of the age is its concern for law and order, not in a reactionary, but in an anticipatory and transformative sense, the quest for a 'Christian order and brotherly unity'.[2]

Johann Metz has reminded us of Walter Benjamin's term, the 'dangerous memory of the people'.[3] Few terms, of course, have

---

[1] *'auff das sich das yrdische leben schwencke in den hymel'*; MSB, p. 281, 30f.

[2] Johannes Locher, *Ein Sendbrief des Bauernfeinds an Karsthans* in *Flugschriften der frühen Reformationsbewegung* ed. Adolf Laube, etc.; Berlin: Akademie Verlag, 1983), vol. 2, p. 965.

[3] Johann Baptist Metz, *Faith in History and Society* (London: Burns & Oates, 1980), pp. 184ff.

been so abused in our abusive century as 'the people', the commune, the Popular Front, *das Volk*. Combined with twisted, selective memories, populism has proved again and again a cruel seducer. Laced with Utopian and millenarian dreams, and exploited by party hierarchies, it has become the stuff of nightmare. Yet when Adam delved and Eve span, who was then the gentleman? Who were the people? How did they relate to the institutional Church in town and country?

The dangerous memories of prophetic and apostolic Scripture flowed deep and fast in early sixteenth-century Europe, like some vast underground river system, mingling with many other tributaries: faint recollections, for example, of half-forgotten folk heroes, sometimes transmogrified into local saints,[4] astonishingly vivid recollections of the Waldensians or John Huss surfacing in art and songs and poetry. It was 'that smothered undercurrent of pain and injustice', as Gordon Rupp put it, which was articulated by preachers such as Thomas Müntzer.[5] Contemporary crises, such as the Diet of Worms, triggered off angry memories of such prophetic figures from the past.

We are aware, today, as a previous generation of historians could not be, of the century-long processes of social, institutional and intellectual change in which the Reformation is embedded. Some of the most recent scholarship on the early Reformation has challenged the view that it was a great upheaval, an *Umbruch*, and some have even argued that the Reformation is in danger of being 'lost', squeezed out between an appreciation of the dynamism of the late Middle Ages and the seminal importance for modernity of the confessional era of the later sixteenth century and beyond.[6]

---

[4]   Cf. David Gentilcore, *From Bishop to Witch. The System of the Sacred in Early Modern Terra d'Otranto* (Manchester and New York: Manchester University Press, 1992).

[5]   'Thomas Müntzer: prophet of radical Christianity', *Bulletin of the John Rylands Library*, 48, reproduced in *Wisdom and Wit*, p. 487.

[6]   *Die frühe Reformation* in *Deutschland als Umbruch*, esp. Heinz Schilling, 'Reformation-Umbruch oder Gipfelpunkt eines Temps des Réformes?', pp. 13–34.

Prophecies of Peasant War: Title page of Practica uber die grossen und
manigfeltigen Coniunction der Planeten . . . *Nuremberg, 1523*

We have already noted that the apocalyptic views which
challenged the symbolic power of the enchanted world, with its
myths of continuity, preceded the Reformation, and that the
anticlericalism which undermined the symbolic power of the
clergy had a long prehistory. It will always be a fine matter of
judgement to balance the competing claims of continuity and
change. However, we have at least to be cautious about certain
tendencies to invest the late medieval period with an aura of

romanticism, which may not be unrelated to the profoundly unrevolutionary mood of the Western world in our own time.

In the last chapter we saw how a new symbolism of freedom, light and the living Word of God had infected popular discourse. Contemporaries certainly believed they were living at a time of unparalleled upheaval or *Umbruch*, which encouraged remarkable dreams of rural and urban transformation. We may have to listen to them more attentively, whatever the current academic fashions prescribe. By focusing on shifts in the imaginative world, the root metaphors in which people articulated their fears and hopes, rather than on institutional or doctrinal history, we may be better able to engage in that listening.

However, if this was an eminently Utopian time, who were the promoters of the dream, who set the agenda for the transformation of countryside and city? In the cities, was it the preachers, the magistrates or the guilds, or did it vary from place to place and time to time, depending on varying constellations of power and civic autonomy, on vulnerability to political pressure or even armed attack? The question of the relationship between 'popular' and 'magisterial' Christianity, of the social significance of the Reformation in the cities and in the countryside, is one of the most lively and controversial debates in current scholarship. Did the cities become 'schools for Christ', transformed by the theologians' programmes, or were the Reformers, clerical and lay, instrumentalised by patricians and patriarchs out for social control? How did women fare in this whole process?[7] Was the Reformation a sacralising process, continuing the medieval tradition of the sacred city, or a secularising one? What was the relationship between city and countryside, between the south west and the more socially conservative north east? In the rural context, from Switzerland to the Tyrol, do we need to take account of a vigorous communal tradition which had its

[7]   A fine recent summary of the situation of women in religion, law and work is Merry E. Wiesner, *Gender, Church and State in Early Modern Germany* (London and New York: Longmans, 1998).

own reforming agendas, and which may have had close connections not only with the Peasants' War, that vast revolutionary
upheaval of 1524–5 which was the greatest in Europe prior to
the French Revolution, but also with the so-called Radical
Reformation?[8]

We like to be simple-minded people, to think of Luther or
Calvin beating a drum and everyone marching along behind them.
We know about leaders such as Zwingli in Zurich, and Bucer in
Strasbourg and Osiander in Nuremberg. We are well informed
about the heroic exiles, mainly single males, who made their way
from England, Scotland, France, Italy and Poland to Geneva. But
what of the little family groups which trudged towards the
Hutterite and other Anabaptist colonies in the east, endangered
every inch of the way, or the pious folk who set out from the Low
Countries for Münster in 1534, hoping to find the New Jerusalem
there?[9] Doctrinal historians have often ignored or marginalised
creative and courageous thinkers such as Hubmaier and Müntzer.
Some, who should know better, continue to demonise them. The
events in Münster in 1535 still tend to be dismissed as an anarchic,
polygamous disaster from beginning to end. But does this tell the
full story? Too often in the past we have been offered a bowdlerised
Reformation, with its revolutionary teeth drawn and lay people
and women adding some colourful touches on the margins. The
good and godly Reformation has been surgically detached from
the Peasants' War and the alleged excesses of the Radicals. Our
social historians, on the other hand, have tended to read the
Reformation as a protracted exercise in patriarchy and social
control. We are caught, it seems, between a materialist reading of
history, which knows so much better than those involved what

---

[8]   Peter Blickle, *The Revolution of 1525. The German Peasants' War from a
New Perspective* (tr. Thomas A. Brady, Jr., and H. C. Erik Midelfort; Baltimore
and London: Johns Hopkins University Press, 1981).
[9]   James Stayer, *The German Peasants' War and Anabaptist Community of
Goods* (Montreal and Kingston; London and Buffalo: McGill-Queen's
University Press, 1991).

they were really on about, and the ethereal essentialism of traditional church history.

Heiko Oberman has suggested a more comprehensive approach, one which acknowledges the fundamental importance of social and economic factors in creating the matrix from which the Reformation springs, but which is aware that until the concerns they throw up are articulated by the preachers and opinion-makers they remain inchoate, amorphous, unable to exert historical leverage.[10] The particular interest of these chapters is to suggest that this articulation is not just on the intellectual level, but is Martin Luther King-like, visionary, carried by the language of dreams. Quite ordinary people read their Psalms and set out for a new Zion. They read the Magnificat and had a hunch that in God's plans there was a place for women and a home for the poor.[11]

Luther really hit a raw nerve when he used the image of the captivity of Babylon, Christendom in exile, in his remarkable 1520 writing about the sacraments. This hugely influential metaphor, already used by the Hussites, encapsulated the sense of alienation, of displacement, the yearning to 'come home'. People sensed that they were living not only between the times, but between Babylon and Zion, between Babel, the confusion of languages, and Pentecost, the reconciliation of discourse. One can hardly over-estimate the importance of the Psalmist's vision of Zion for the Reformers, the concreteness with which a psalm such as Psalm 48 would be read: the city of God with its palaces and towers, its courts of justice, its temple, its ramparts.[12] In the papal kingdom, Karlstadt said, we are held captive like the Jews in Babylon, deprived not only of the substance of life, but of the Word of God itself.[13] Lay people wanted their village, their town, to ring to the

---

[10]   Heiko A. Oberman, *The Impact of the Reformation* (Edinburgh: T. & T. Clark, 1994), esp. pp. vii–xi.

[11]   Cf. Werner O. Packull, *Hutterite Beginnings*.

[12]   Cf. Psalms 6, 20, 46, 50, 76, 87, 99, 122, 137.

[13]   *The Essential Carlstadt*, p. 50.

Psalms of Zion, but also to incarnate the righteousness of the prophets so they could follow their Captain (*hauptmann*) Christ right into the interstices of day-to-day life. Popular revolts would be preceded by processions carrying a crucifix or a red cross and a naked sword.[14] The pervasiveness of the covenantal motif in the writings of Johann Eberlin von Günzburg, Zwingli, Müntzer and others reflects this concern.[15]

In the midst of the Peasants' War the peasants from Sangerhausen in Thuringia wrote:

> We poor country folk from the villages of the whole district of Sangerhausen . . . have vowed and sworn a divine covenant, in the love of God and the holy gospel, being ready to offer up our bodies and lives for it.[16]

The motif or image of the covenant, often closely associated with the Bible as the Old and New Covenants, was in fact one of the most powerful and pervasive in these years. The divine covenant forged together the vision of heaven and the realities of earth. Once again the people of God were marching out of captivity to a promised land. The aim of the divine or eternal leagues signed at Allstedt and Mühlhausen was to restore the divine ordering of life, the *ordo rerum*. The assumption of the lords and princes that all created life belonged to them was the root of the problem. 'There is no greater abomination on earth than the fact that no one is prepared to take up the cause of the needy.'[17]

It is true that there is frequently tension between the divine justification for the covenant, as a defensive league to prevent the suppression of the Gospel, and much more down-to-earth

---

[14] As in Mühlhausen; Scott, *Thomas Müntzer*, pp. 111–14.

[15] An interesting treatment of this is by Thomas Kaufman, 'Anonyme Flugschriften der frühen Reformation', in *Die frühe Reformation in Deutschland als Umbruch* (ed. Bernd Moeller, with Stephen E. Buckwalter; Gütersloh: Gütersloher Verlagshaus, 1998), pp. 191–267, esp. pp. 239–51.

[16] CW, p. 146.

[17] CW, p. 335.

concerns for access to forests or rivers or common grazing.[18] But where egalitarian yearnings surfaced, they were invariably couched in biblical terms. The aim was to make 'all Christians equal', to hold all things in common.[19] The great symbols of injustice, the castles and monasteries, were to be razed to the ground.

Moreover, the covenant came to be seen as a commitment to God and to 'love each other as brothers'[20] which transcended all mere political loyalties. For Müntzer, godly government, as opposed to mere tyranny, rested on the presupposition that the ruler was bound in covenant to God and to God's elect. The leagues or covenants developed a paramilitary role, because a régime which did not defend its people from, for example, persecution for their loyalty to God forfeited its right to rule and should be overturned by the covenanters, the angels or saints of God.[21] This would be a justified uprising, for the princes were given by God to be servants of the sword, not lords over it.[22] Fear of God, and one's oath before God and the elect, must drive out all other fears. This was the precondition for true progress, reform, *besserung*, taking place.[23] The covenant is one of the most potent examples of a central biblical paradigm taking hold of the political imagination. It humanised and personalised politics by making government accountable. Its direct commitment of the people to God relativised the authority of the ruler, and introduced a voluntarist dimension to the political realm which often corresponded to a predilection for adult baptism in the ecclesiastical realm.

The Utopian thrust in politics was not restricted, however, to this covenantal expression. There is a much more widespread

[18]   CW, pp. 102f.

[19]   CW, pp. 436f.; caution is in place in interpreting such statements made under torture.

[20]   As Claus Rautenzweig, a member of Müntzer's Allstedt League, put it; AGBMII, p. 453; quoted by Scott, *Thomas Müntzer*, p. 172.

[21]   CW, p. 117.

[22]   CW, pp. 132f.

[23]   CW, pp. 114f.

assumption that the city or commune was itself sacred. In his now classical book on the German imperial cities, Bernd Moeller opened up a dramatic window on what we might call the sacred city, the communal roots of the Reformation in the urban context. For at least two decades now, Italian Renaissance historians have also been drawing attention to the secular pursuit of holiness, models of sanctity drawn not from ascetic or reclusive life but from the innocence of children, for example.[24] What one might call a theology of creation developed, based on a burgeoning patristic scholarship; an awareness that our *humanitas* rested precisely on the divine image within us and was a gift of divine grace. This led to an appreciation of the vocation to ordinary life, and in particular to civic service. In a figure such as Gasparo Contarini, later one of the leaders of Catholic reform and an almost exact contemporary of Luther, a deeply eucharistic and Augustinian piety is combined with a conscious decision not to join his friends entering the reclusive Camaldolensian order, but to serve God 'without the cowl' by devoting himself to the common good of the republic of Venice as a consecrated public servant and diplomat.[25]

This sense of the commonalty, the commonwealth, the commune as constituting sacred community, is fundamental to an understanding of the Reformation. It could, and often did, lead to a romanticisation and idealisation of the harmony, continuity and concord of the republic. It had conservative manifestations: the concern to avoid any challenge to traditional deferences and structures of power and to safeguard law and order. The latter was essential for cities whose prosperity rested on trade. Lawlessness was a menace for all citizens. Artisans cursed

---

[24]   Bernd Moeller, *Imperial Cities and the Reformation* (tr. and ed. H. C. Eric Midelfort and Mark Edwards, Jr.; Philadelphia: Fortress Press, 1972). *The Pursuit of Holiness in Late Medieval and Renaissance Religion* (ed. Charles Trinkaus and Heiko A. Oberman, Leiden: Brill, 1974).

[25]   Elisabeth G. Gleason, *Gasparo Contarini. Venice, Rome and Reform* (Berkeley, Los Angeles and Oxford: University of California Press, 1993).

rampaging knights and robber bands. For the Protestant cities the Old Testament guidelines for society meant that rulers had a *cura religionis*, the duty to preserve and extend truth and repress error. Moses, after all, was 'the best republican'. This was no revolutionary dream. But there is a strong ethic of service. Princes or magistrates were there for the good and needs of others, not for themselves, and ultimate accountability was, for both subject and ruler, to God and his holy Word.

After the upheavals of the Peasants' War, traumatised civic leaders insisted that purely theological considerations had to be balanced by the need to hold the community together. As Jacob Sturm, the Strasbourg patrician put it: 'as members of one body . . . we should . . . display love for one another'. Some sense of perspective was required. 'Both sides [Catholics and Evangelicals] are Christians, however, may God have mercy.'[26] It might be necessary to censor the writings of hotheads, and not – for example – to abolish the Mass prematurely or to absolutise a particular understanding of the Eucharist. The Eucharist re-emerged in such thought patterns as social cement; reform as an antidote to revolution. In many instances, particularly in rural communities, communes united to defend the Mass and traditional church polity against innovative city slickers. In divided urban communities the disputations functioned not only as a way to discover the truth of the Gospel but to find a tolerant consensus which safeguarded the peace of the city.

For a patrician such as Sturm, the adoption of evangelical views had meant leaving the priesthood to serve the city as a privy councillor and diplomat. This secular but religiously motivated ministry involved him during the Peasants' War in highly risky visits to the camps of the peasant rebels, and later in endlessly shuttling back and forth to the territorial or imperial diets, trying

---

[26]   Thomas Brady, '"Sind also zu beiden theilen Christen, des Gott erbarm." Le mémoire de Jacques Sturm sur le culte publique à Strasbourg (août 1525)', in *Horizons européens de la Réforme en Alsace . . .* (Strasbourg: Librairie Istra, 1980), pp. 75–7, lines 76–99; cited in Brady, *Protestant Politics . . .* , p. 60.

to form an effective alliance to defend Protestant interests as well as Strasbourg's. His was a prudential vision, with criteria of 'doability' and meritocracy, a judicious Jerusalem rather than an enchanted one. His godly society, like that of the extraordinary Katharina Schutz Zell, with her hospitality and non-dogmatic spirit, exhibited the fruits of love in kindness, generosity and compassion for the suffering. For Zell, who to all intents and purposes acted like a pastor herself, the chief aim was *besserung*, improvement in personal and social life, not endless disputes about doctrine or refinements of cult.[27] It was not an individualistic religious vision, but one which embraced the whole community.

J. H. Hexter pointed out many years ago that what attracted so many humanists to Calvinism was that it seemed to offer a practical way to implement such Utopian dreams.[28] Despite decades of scholarship, our stubborn mental block about thinking of humanism and Calvinism together (humanism being 'progressive', Calvinism 'reactionary') illustrates the difficulty of the territory we shall be traversing, pockmarked with exhausted hermeneutical mineshafts and all manner of traps for the unwary. The adventure of reconstructing the dangerous memory of the *laos*, *le peuple*, *das gemeine volk*, tempts some of us to romanticism, others to exaggerated caution. And we like to think monocausally. We don't digest alliances easily. But the revolution we call the Reformation was one long succession of alliances.

The plethora of competing Utopias in our period, princely and urban, feudal and communal, national, regional and local, not to mention the universalist Utopias of pope and emperor and the ancient, stubborn dreams of the monastic orders and the universities, were all elbowing for space in the collective consciousness. Some, like the phenomenally unpopular friars, were characterised

---

[27]   Cf. Elsie Anne McKee, *The Writings of Katharina Schütz Zell:*. Vol. I *Interpretation*; Vol. II *A Critical Edition* (Leiden: Brill, 1998).

[28]   'Utopia and Geneva', in *Action and Conviction in Early Modern Europe: Essays in Memory of E. H. Herbison* (ed. T. K. Robb and J. E. Siegel; Princeton: Princeton University Press, 1969), pp. 77–89.

as vermin, gnats, locusts, wasps, gnawing away at the noble grain of God's Word, apparently heading for relegation,[29] while others were heading for promotion to the premier league.[30] The hectic pamphlet warfare of the early 1520s reflected this struggle for the cultural high ground.

Closely associated with the battle for the mind was the battle for power. The reformations of the sixteenth century may best be seen, not as competitors with many of these Utopias, but as partners, as allies in their attempts to earth themselves. Theologians such as Martin Bucer had their visions, but so did lay people such as Jacob Sturm. As the history of Strasbourg might suggest, it could take the whole century for a new balance of interests to emerge. Not surprisingly, perhaps, the laity won some of the battles, the Protestant clergy, others. Alliances are like that.[31]

Chrisman's closely researched study of more than a hundred lay writers, *Conflicting Visions of Reform*, makes the point that lay people had very clear agendas of their own which differed according to whether they were princes, peasants, artisans, professionals or patricians. Her approach is much more helpful than that of those who attempt to characterise lay attitudes in a generic way. But for all lay people certain power issues tended to recur: Who had the right to pronounce excommunication, to hear confessions, to oversee wills, to formulate prayers? It was not just the priests or theologians of the Old Church who frustrated the desire of lay people to have control over their own spirituality. On occasion, for example, evangelical clergy tried to inhibit lay people from introducing their own spontaneous prayers into worship.[32] Virtually every Protestant city saw protracted tussles between magistrates and ministers.

[29]   Chrisman, *Conflicting Visions*, p. 143.
[30]   Geoffrey Dipple, *Antifraternalism and Anticlericalism in the German Reformation. Johann Eberlin von Günzburg and the Campaign against the Friars* (Aldershot: Scolar Press, 1996).
[31]   Abray, *The People's Reformation*, esp. chs 8 and 9.
[32]   Chrisman, *Conflicting Visions*, pp. 172f., 175, 189, 195, 218.

The tension between the populist ideal and the emergent oligarchical forms of civic government has been perspicaciously analysed by Thomas Brady. He has drawn attention to the importance of the Swiss republican model. A popular proverb had it that 'when a cow stood on the bridge at Ulm and mooed, she'd be heard in the middle of Switzerland'.[33] Would the new reforming cities of Southern Germany 'turn Swiss', forge a political as well as theological alliance with the republican and communal traditions of the Swiss and tend towards a theocracy? Or would they edge towards a more hierarchical style of polity, seeing the Kingdom of God in more spiritual terms and finding congenial partners in the Protestant princes?

At first, what one might call the patriarchal and prophetic streams of Hebrew tradition were able to coexist in cities such as Strasbourg and Augsburg, as patricians and populace alike were attracted to the reforming message. Preachers sought to commend both to city councils and congregations their conviction that the common good was one and the same as the *lex Christi*. The communal ideal and the scriptural plumb-line seemed to be one and the same and carrying everything before them. Indeed, the momentum of the reforming demands in the early 1520s for a more accountable clergy, a more educated laity and an enlightened piety made cities virtually ungovernable until their councils had offered concession after concession to them. This was despite their prudential concern to maintain good relations with the emperor, their traditional ally against the territorial princes, by respecting the prohibition by the Edict of Worms in 1521 of any such religious innovations of this kind. Step by step they found themselves moving from the accustomed business of appointing civic preachers and organising hospitals to legislating about doctrine and morality as a whole, abolishing begging and organising a viable welfare system. As Brady says, these reforming

---

[33] Thomas A. Brady, *Turning Swiss: Cities and Empire, 1450–1550* (Cambridge Studies in Early Modern History; Cambridge University Press, 1985), p. 39.

measures should be seen 'less as inevitable products of individual politicians' conversions than as actions of urban governments'.[34]

This is no pietistic, individualist Protestantism. In the *Appeal to the German Nobility* and countless other statements and writings, Luther and his followers undergirded the traditional *gravamina* or complaints of the German Estates with biblical principles. Zwingli and his allies and followers took it for granted that the whole of life was to be remoulded by the Gospel. Argula von Grumbach's writing to the Bavarian princes in 1523 is an excellent example of how a lay person saw the resort to Holy Scripture transforming political, social and cultural life.[35] For lay people, issues of social and personal ethics were inseparable from those of salvation.[36] The concern for the public good 'gave even the forms of piety a public relevance'.[37]

'The common man is thirsting now everywhere for God's Word and the Gospel.' This is the kind of fiery language often used by Thomas Müntzer and other radicals. But it was in fact uttered by the douce representatives of the cities at the Diet of Nuremberg in early 1524, when explaining to the emperor why any attempt to enforce the edict of the Diet of Worms would lead to a total breakdown in law and order.[38] Town clerks such as Spengler of Nuremberg saw the Word of God as racing through territory after territory, town after town and, in the metaphor of the time, taking firm root. Freedom, justice, and truth would surely prevail. Civic disputations between Reformers and conservatives, like that in Nuremberg in 1525, led to the old ways being publicly and humiliatingly discredited. Apocalypse now!

---

[34]   Brady, *Turning Swiss*, p. 158.
[35]   *A Christian Writing by an honourable noblewoman* . . . in AvG, pp. 96–112.
[36]   Heinrich Robert Schmidt, 'Die Ethik der Laien in der Reformation', *Die frühe Reformation in Deutschland als Umbruch*, pp. 333–70.
[37]   Heiko A. Oberman, *Masters of the Reformation: The Emergence of a New Intellectual Climate in Europe* (tr. Dennis Martin; Cambridge, 1981), p. 188.
[38]   RTA JR 4: 506–8, no. 113, quoted in Brady, *Turning Swiss*, pp. 168f.

The popularity and prevalence of the disputation, in which contentious religious issues were decided not by bishops or synods, but with Scripture as judge and city council as jury, assumed the autonomy of the sacred city. Communal–federal dreams were almost unquestioningly linked with biblical–covenantal paradigms – reminiscent of nineteenth-century missionaries assuming the nexus of Christianity and civilisation.

All this suggests that the view that, '*grosso modo*', the early Reformation was simply Luther writ large, cannot stand. The civic reformers filtered out of Luther what suited them. They learned massively from his teachings and example, but married his principles with their own communal visions and traditions. Made wary by what they conceived to be predatory bishops and privileged clerics in the past, they were determined that the new pastors would be less numerous, less expensive, servants and not masters, no longer uniquely privileged as mediators between humanity and God, but learned teachers and caring shepherds. As the great medieval preacher in Strasbourg, Johann Geiler von Kayserberg, speaking of all leaders, political and ecclesiastical, had said: 'The communes do not exist for their sake, but they for the commune's sake.'[39]

Yet from the beginning there was tension. Patricians and guilds interpreted the communal ideal differently. Chrisman argues that artisans never used the term 'the common good' for this very reason.[40] They preferred to speak of championing the interests of the poor. They wanted social as well as ecclesiastical reform, and did not want to be called Lutheran. They preferred the term 'evangelical'. The pastors were often caught in the middle. The Strasbourg or Nuremberg pastors, for example, tended to operate as a collective group, almost a caste, as teachers, preachers,

---

[39] *Die emeis: dis ist das buch von der Omeissen, und auch Herr der könnig ich diente gern* (Strasbourg: Johann Grüninger, 1516), 8v–9v, quoted in Brady, *Protestant Politics*, p. 25.

[40] Though it was used elsewhere in a positive sense by peasant radicals such as Gaismair or Hergot; Chrisman, *Conflicting Visions*, pp. 181, 186.

prophets, discipliners, carers. With salaries of about 100 gulden a year they were highly esteemed, ranking socially just after the patricians. From the beginning this select core of city preachers sought to exercise quality control over their rural brothers' life and doctrine.[41] It was not only Calvin who took himself and his prophetic office with such solemn seriousness! Much more research needs to be given to the relationships between the ordained clergy, their networking through meetings and correspondence, their pastoral care for one another, the fascinating roles of pastors' wives such as Katharina Schütz Zell, their alliances with city clerks, teachers and publishers. Their professional interests were not necessarily identical with those of the poor, any more than with the patrician leaders.

No one doubts any longer the importance of the towns for the reception and spread of the Reformation. Germany, however, around 1500 was a patchwork of some 350 competing jurisdictions. The eye may be caught initially by the famous imperial cities such as Augsburg or Regensburg, or the vast episcopal territories, especially on the Rhine, or the great principalities: Bavaria, Saxony, Hesse. We have been reminded by Volker Press and others in recent years, however, of the continuing importance of the nobility, including the lesser nobility, with their networks, the *Ritterbunde* in Wurttemberg, Saxony and Franconia.[42] What would the early Reformation have been without Ulrich von Hutten or Franz von Sickingen? The imperial knights, as Press has shown, were one aspect of a much larger problem, caught between the rising power of state-builders on one side and the imperial fantasies of the Habsburgs and the papacy on the other. They were not just thugs in armour. The lesser nobility had

[41]   Cf. Heinz Dannenbauer, 'Die Nürnberger Landesgeistlichen bis zur zweiten Nürnberger Kirchenvisitation (1560/61). Ergänzungen zu Würfels "Diptycha Ecclesiarum in oppidis et pagis Norimbergensibus"', *Zeitschrift für Bayerische Kirchengeschichte* 2 (1927), pp. 207–36.

[42]   Cf. Volker Press, 'Wilhelm von Grumbach und die deutsche Adelskrise', *Blätter für deutsche Landesgeschichte*, vol. 113 (1997), pp. 396–431.

genuine grievances. How were their 'freedoms', their culture of feuding, their legal rights, to be preserved in a new age? Cowboys on a lost frontier!

Recently, Miriam Chrisman has highlighted their contribution to the undermining of the whole clerical establishment. Their attack on papal tyranny was also an impressive plea for freedom of speech; Christ was never secretive, they insisted; why, after all, did he send out the Holy Spirit? Everything rests on 'the mouth of the truth of Christ', Sickingen said, a powerful image indeed. The 'evangelical Christian discourse' at the Ebernburg, Franz von Sickingen's castle, conducted by luminaries such as Oecolampadius, the later reformer of Basel, led the Pforzheim reformer Johannes Schwöbel to write 'Now it is necessary to go to school to the laity and learn to read the Bible from them.'[43]

When we come to the rural scene, we have to remember, of course, that urban dynamism was very dependent on its regional hinterland. The walls around the early modern city give us the wrong message. All towns leaked into the countryside in a way we can hardly conceive of today: the traffic to the vineyards on the surrounding hills, the in and out of cattle and people, the links created by kinship, legal, trading and religious networks, social and financial obligations. Interconnections between great cities such as Nuremberg and their satellite towns and villages were an infinitely complex mixture of *realpolitik*, concerned with defending vital spheres of influence, and a genuine sense of responsibility for the bodies and souls of their outlying subjects.

Peter Blickle and his school have stimulated scholarship in recent years by his thesis that the first form taken by the Reformation in the villages of the south west of Germany was a

---

[43]   Cf. his preface to Sickingen's *Sendbrieff . . . dem Junckherr Diethern von Henschüchsheim*, cited by Miriam Usher Chrisman, *Conflicting Visions*, p. 69; cf. pp. 54, 79. Cf. Hans-Jürgen Goertz, 'Adel versus Klerus. Antiklerikale Polemik in Flugschriften des Adels', in Goerz, *Antiklerikalismus und Reformation* (Göttingen, 1995), pp. 45–65.

popular, communal one.[44] The reception of Luther's ideas fused with the pervasive concern for a new ordering of the whole of society. Ecclesiastical or spiritual concerns such as those for the free preaching of Scripture and the right of communities to appoint their own pastor were quite inseparable from social and political ones. The divine law, as articulated in Genesis 1.28–29 for example, was seen as undergirding customary rights: the dominion over land and sea and all that grew there. This communal reformation, Blickle argues, flowed into the Peasants' War, to be superceded by the more conservative and centralising magisterial reformation after the war.

There is certainly a growing body of evidence from Switzerland, the Tyrol, even distant Scotland and the mountain regions of Italy,[45] that disenchantment with friars and oppressive feudal monasteries was often accompanied by a fervent wish to encourage a good parish ministry, to support the church and the churchyard as the hub of communal gathering and identity. Outside rural society there is a growing awareness of the foundational role of peasants in society and the need to take account of their interests.

The revolutionary Hussite traditions had encouraged similar ideas, and they were reflected in the extraordinary popularity of the largely anonymous pamphlets of the early 1520s in which peasants emerged as the archetypal champions of the new faith. This is an extraordinary reversal, as peasants had hitherto been ridiculed by the literati. Figures such as the peasant spokesman Karsthans brandishing his flail – echoes of Christ in the Temple – are now portrayed as the best exemplars of biblical Christianity. There are hints that a new awareness of the dignity of the peasant was developing, as in Jacob Wimpheling's Prayer of the Common

[44]   Peter Blickle, *Communal Salvation – the question for salvation in sixteenth-century Germany* (tr. Thomas Dunlap; Atlantic Highlands, NJ, and London: Humanities Press, 1992).

[45]   As suggested in a recent lecture by Professor Sam Cohn, 'The Religiosity of Mountain People in Renaissance Florence', at the Society for Renaissance Studies, meeting in Edinburgh, 9 May 1998.

Folk to God, 'who nourish the whole of society and in return have only their poverty'.[46] The peasant was now praised as the backbone of a healthy, communal life. One suspects there may be a throwback to ideas of Adamic innocence. A pamphleteer such as Argula von Grumbach also noted that Jesus, his disciples, the women around him and the apostles and prophets were simple folk. 'Who were the apostles – after all? What higher learning could they recall?'[47] The idealised figure of the simple, honest peasant was promoted in these humanist dialogues as an 'Every-man' figure, untrammelled by the usual social and professional conflicts of interests, and representative therefore of the whole of humanity.[48] There was an awareness, too, that, as the pervasive metaphor puts it, the peasants were 'flayed and fleeced', 'shackled and fettered', 'poor, care-worn folk' who 'have spent their life in a grim struggle for bread in order to fill the throats of the most godless tyrants'. Their material poverty and lack of sophistication meant that they were more likely to be poor in spirit, to risk all to be true disciples of Christ, but their oppressed life-style left them scant time for spiritual matters.[49] On his death-bed, the Elector Frederick the Wise, conservative as he was, wondered if the tribulations of the Peasants' War were a divine retribution for the long history of abuse of the 'common folk'. It might be God's will that the common man take over the reins of power.[50]

James Stayer and others have demonstrated that the original concern of the Swiss Brethren, the first Anabaptists, was for a

[46] *Jacob Wimpheling, Opera Selecta* 3:112; quoted by Brady, *Protestant Politics*, p. 31.

[47] AvG, p. 177.

[48] Thomas Kaufmann has made the important and, to my knowledge, novel point that the anonymity of many of the early Reformation pamphlets suggested a claim to universal validity, '*universale Wahrheitsrepräsentanz*'. 'Anonyme Flugschriften der frühen Reformation', in *Die frühe Reformation in Deutschland als Umbruch*, pp. 191–267.

[49] CW, p. 294.

[50] AGBM II. P. 91; quoted by Goertz, *Antiklerikalismus und Reformation*, p. 148.

communal reformation, to renew the entire community as the congregation of Christ. The separatist, free church character of Anabaptism only came to the fore after the failure to achieve the initial aims.[51] Werner Packull has documented that support for Hutter's Anabaptists in the Tyrol had a similar grass-roots character.[52]

The Blickle thesis remains, however, hotly debated. Was there any real community of interest between city-dwellers and the peasants? Frequently, as at Mühlhausen in 1524 for example, where its seventeen villages abstained from the communal opposition, we can see them at odds with one another.[53] Is not the picture of communal solidarity an idealised one? Tom Scott has pointed out that many if not most of the communal concerns for the accountability of clergy and justice for ordinary folk could have been accommodated within a reformed but orthodox Catholic ecclesiology. Were they really Reformation concerns at all, except perhaps where the monopoly of the priesthood on the mediation of the divine was so blatant that it provoked an overwhelming anticlerical reaction?[54] The point is well taken if doctrinal criteria such as justification by faith are used to define the Reformation. If, however, as I have been arguing, we are talking about paradigm shifts in the understanding of Christianity which involved a multiplicity of alliances of evangelical concerns with patricians, artisans and imperial knights, as well as villagers, then some of the concerns of Scott and others may be met.

[51]   Stayer first developed this argument in 'Die Anfänge des Schweizerischen Täufertums im Kongregationalismus', in *Umstrittenes Täufertum, 1525–1975. Neue Forschungen* (ed. Hans-Jürgen Goertz; Göttingen: Vandenhoeck & Ruprecht, 1975), pp. 19–49.

[52]   Packull, *Hutterite Beginnings*, pp. 161–86.

[53]   Scott, *Thomas Müntzer*, pp. 120f.

[54]   Tom Scott, 'The Communal Reformation between Town and Country', in *Archiv für Reformationsgeschichte. Sonderband: Die Reformation in Deutschland und Europa: Interpretationen und Debatten* (ed. Hans R. Guggisberg and Gottfried G. Krodel; Gütersloh: Gütersloher Verlagshaus, 1993), pp. 175–92.

Petrarca Meister. Tree of Estates in Society, *1519/20*

Albrecht Dürer. John the Baptist

The theory of a radical communal reformation gains support from an unexpected quarter: the world of art. The previously despised and caricatured peasants were vividly and sympathetically depicted by a formidable group of artists, including Dürer, Till Riemenschneider, Lucas Cranach, Urs Graf, Jörg Ratgeb, Matthew Grünewald, Nicklaus Manuel. The image of the peasant 'captured' the art world. The so-called 'Petrarca Meister' has the peasants carrying the whole world on their backs; the great roots of the tree on which the various estates of society perch are so interwoven with the figures of two peasants as to be indistinguishable from them, and at the summit of the tree, again, two peasants are sitting.[55] Whether at dance, at work or, like Dürer's peasant woman, in tears, they emerge with a new-found dignity which is paralleled by their prominent role in Reformation dialogues and pamphlets. When Dürer wants to show John the Baptist preaching it is to an audience of ordinary folk, including women and children, in the woods on the margins of civilised society. Children and women are also prominent in the etchings of the Behaim brothers, members of the youth culture, who were expelled from Nuremberg as being 'godless painters', suspect of Anabaptism.

Perhaps most remarkable of all, however, are the depictions of Christ and his disciples in Grünewald's altar-pieces, and the sensationally powerful work of Jörg Ratgeb, still all too little known in the English-speaking world.[56] Here we gain a window into the common folk's vision of the liberating Christ who identified himself with their suffering, and his earthy disciples. It is reminiscent of Pasolini's film version of the Gospel of St Matthew. The Last Supper becomes again the rough and ready meal it once was. The crude manners and features of the disciples

[55] Petrarca Meister: Ständebaum, *Bauern und Künstler. Die Künstler der Renaissance und der Bauernkrieg von 1525* (tr. Tilly Bergner; Berlin: Henschelverlag, 1961), p. 63.

[56] Wilhelm Fraenger, *Jörg Ratgeb. Ein Maler und Märtyrer aus dem Bauernkrieg* (Dresden: VEB Verlag der Kunst, 1972).

Hans Weiditz. Peasant Dancers, c. *1521*

remind the onlooker of the kind of company Jesus chose to keep.
The realities of the crucifixion are mercilessly portrayed. Yet, in
Ratgeb's paintings as in those of other artists dealing with the
'peasant Christ', the Easter lamb with the flag of victory is also
prominent. This same Christ will lead them, the weak and
oppressed, to triumph in the end.

The flags used during the Peasants' War are interesting. Jesus,
Mary and John would often be depicted on one side but, instead

Lucas Cranach, the Older. Peasant Huntsman, c. *1515*

of the kneeling aristocratic patron, a peasant accompanied them, while on the other side the *bundschuh*, or boot, the revolutionary symbol of the peasant, waved proudly in the air.[57] Or they featured Christ as the sole mediator, with the Lutheran slogan, '*Verbum*

[57] Hans-Sebald Behaim spread knowledge about Grünewald's populist Christ in pamphlet form: Maurice Pianzola, *Bauern und Künstler*, pp. 77, 112.

Domini Manet in Eternum'. The Word of God abides to all eternity.

Thus the Peasants' War, as Stayer has argued, may have been the form in which the Reformation was received in many South German villages.[58] Christ, as the third article of the most famous peasant manifesto, the Twelve Articles, said, has 'redeemed us and bought us all by the shedding of his precious blood . . . Therefore it is demonstrated by Scripture that we are free and wish to be free'.[59] For the peasants and artisans involved in the war, the good news of the Gospel was not justification by faith or theories about the sacraments, but a divine ordinance which offered them dignity and freedom, vernacular worship, access to the sacraments and caring pastors. This was the purity of Scripture, this was salvation: a transformed society. Access to salvation, leaders such as Müntzer insisted, also meant access to the good gifts of creation. In the past the peasants had been robbed both of Scripture and of justice. Now, as the Mühlhausen Articles declared, the poor should be treated as well as the rich. There should be one law for everyone. As the Klettgauers put it, 'there is no true judge in heaven or on earth other than the Word of God'.[60]

In the Tyrol campaign Michael Gaismair called for all city walls to be broken down, so that demarcations and divisions between people would be removed. All would become villagers.[61] The removal of religious images was part of this levelling campaign, because they were seen as the legitimisation of privilege and hierarchy. Once again we see that the iconoclasm of the Reformation was not just a concern to remove superfluity and 'stubble', but was complemented if not overshadowed by its

---

[58]   James Stayer, *The German Peasants' War*, p. 43.

[59]   Scott and Scribner, *The German Peasants' War*, p. 254.

[60]   Peter Blickle, 'Zürich's Anteil am deutschen Bauernkrieg. Die Vorstellung des göttlichen Rechts im Klettgau', *Zeitschrift für die Geschichte des Oberrheins* 133 (1985), pp. 81–101; cited Stayer, *The German Peasants' War*, p. 38.

[61]   Ibid., p. 55.

iconopoesis, its vision of a human world which mirrored the divine in its banal, day-to-day reality.

The various Articles of the Peasants in 1525 massively document this communalist conviction that grace, faith, the Gospel, peace, love and concord have to be 'cashed out' in terms of the whole of life, of taxes and tithes and dues, usury and the burden of debt. Johannes Locher believes he is the 'comforter of the peasants' (*baurntröster*) because he bases himself on Scripture and reason and acts as if 'the old Christ still lives'.[62] There was a burning concern for the dignity of life and labour, for freedom from serfdom. Spiritual freedom and personal freedom were inseparable. No other issue was so pervasive in the various articles from Southern Germany as that of serfdom: the right to be one's own person, to marry as one chose, to move to another area, to name one's heirs. The dignity of the Christian in baptism, so lyrically proclaimed by Luther, was given a communal twist. The Word of God freed the conscience but also liberated those in bondage. All were to be brothers, bought by the precious blood of Jesus, and to love one another as brothers.

We cannot, therefore, surgically detach the Reformation from the Peasants' War, this revolution of 1524–5, or at least, if we do so, we are flying in the face of considerable evidence. The peasants saw themselves as true Christians, described themselves as forming Christian Unions or Leagues, and covenanted together in a way very familiar to those of us versed in Scottish traditions. They, too, were 'Covenanters'. James Stayer has shown how this 'Social Gospel', as he calls it, largely based in rural or semi-rural communities, was widely propagated during the Peasants' War. He argues that in its early months, till the end of March 1525, the peasant groupings were generally pacific and concerned to negotiate with the authorities. Their articles had precisely this function.[63] Blickle has pointed to the semi-political nature which

---

[62] *Sendbrief des Bauernfeinds an Karsthans*, pp. 965/4f., 972/3.
[63] Ibid., p. 60.

the peasant hordes or 'Christian Associations' developed as they sought to put Christian brotherly love into practice.[64]

One would be hard put to it, on the other hand, to argue that the radical reformers had a clear vision of the future society which they wished to create. It seems clear that Thomas Müntzer, for example, initially at least, entertained Davidic models of the godly ruler based on the Old Testament, combining this with a popular mysticism, an advocacy of *gelassenheit*. His followers were urged to let go of their attachments to personal property and security. There are unworldly dimensions to this which could have led to social passivity. However, they clearly did not, and the apocalyptic elements in his reading of Scripture and society came to predominate. We have, of course, only fragmentary glimpses of his dream that all things should be in common.[65] But disciples of his such as Hans Hut and Hans Hergot suggest a much larger concern, which was also partly picked up by Hutterite Anabaptism, to recover the apostolic praxis of Acts 2 and 4 and develop a rejuvenated Christian socialism. All would eat from the one bowl, work and live for the common good. Mystical detachment from personal property was combined with a commitment to sharing life, property, even children with one another. In this way the 'dangerous memory of the people' stretched right back a millennium and a half to the New Testament beginnings to challenge the burgeoning market economy of early capitalism. Biblical themes of creation and exodus, stewardship and liberation, Zion and the New Jerusalem and the ancient covenants ignited with contemporary yearnings for peace and justice. The moral imagination was kindled. Political agendas were forged. The horizon flared with the transcendent vision of shalom.

---

[64]   *The Revolution of 1525*, p. 189.

[65]   We may have gone too far in minimising the social and political concerns of Müntzer. Cf. my article 'The Cornflower in the Wheatfield: Freedom and Liberation in Thomas Müntzer (*Archiv für Reformationsgeschichte*), 89 (1998), pp. 41–54, esp. pp. 50f.

CHAPTER FOUR

NIGHTMARE

Pigs had a great life of it, the sixteenth century agreed. Not a worry in the world, just eating their slop and wallowing around in the amiable mud.[1] No nightmares. But then no notable flights of the imagination either.

On the other hand, if you set your face towards Utopia you can expect to be mauled in the process. Success, as Martin Buber loved to repeat, is not one of the names of God. Imaginative courage always exacts its tribute. When a 'great shattering' takes place and an enchanted world is lost, it can free us up to step out in new directions but can also toss us into the abyss. Dreams and nightmares frequently interweave. There is a nightmare dimension to the Reformation, too. Luther's reforming career is bracketed by works of rare lyrical quality, mainly at the beginning, and by staggeringly crude anti-Jewish and anti-papal tracts, mainly at the end. Is this the cost that always has to be paid for the grandiose vision, what always happens when dream, vision and imaginative Utopia stumble against the implacable obstacles of human failings and structural weaknesses? Arthur Koestler talked of the gods failing us with reference to the betrayal of hopes by Stalinist communism.[2] The markers of such crises of identity are depression, despair, hate, resignation and the quest for the scapegoat.

---

[1] Cf. for example Luther's comments. LW 23, p. 291.

[2] *The God that Failed: Six Studies in Communism* (London: Hamish Hamilton, 1950).

There may perhaps be no access to the heritage of the Reformation until we come to terms with its nightmarish dimensions – its divisiveness and destructive polemic, for example. It is not acceptable that central issues such as the witch-hunt or the drift into confessional warfare tend to be left to historians of culture and kept outside the purview of the church historian. Some 30,000 witches, the great majority women, died in the witch-craze. Religious intolerance was manifested in fierce disputes about doctrine and sharp controls on publishing and freedom of speech. Religious massacres and religious wars became the order of the day for more than a hundred years. Why did the great hopes for *besserung*, for liberation from evil, death and sin, appear to have ended like this?

It may be that we have thought too little about the way in which quite contradictory movements can coexist within the one religious landscape. Images of light and liberation can alternate with the blackest nights of the soul. And of course such tensions or conflicts are fought out on many different levels: spiritual, intellectual, social, political. The inmost sanctum of prayer and personal conscience can be lit up by poetry, music, a thousand flickering candles of the imagination; but at the same time a formidable array of purely intellectual arguments may undergird such piety; almost irresistible social pressures support it; and blasphemy laws or acts of uniformity fence it around with legal sanctions of the most draconian nature.

In the previous chapter we have referred to the alliances which were forged between theological insights and whole batteries of competing Utopias, as the battle for the mind and the battle for power were joined. The poets, artists, thinkers and dreamers who relied on the power of the imagination may have trusted in its creativity, but what happened when their advocacy of justice, freedom, light, covenantal values and the living Word of God subverted the academy, encouraged insubordinate attitudes to the magistrate or the magisterium, urged the obsolescence of private property and questioned gender roles?

In Balthasar Stanberger's pamphlet of 1523, for example, papal authority is imaginatively toppled in a genial fantasy which transcended space and time in a manner reminiscent of today's science fiction. St Peter is made to appear chatting to a peasant, and revealing to the astonished fellow that he had never even been in Rome, far less founded the papacy, and that he was 'just a simple chappie'.[3] At a stroke a whole constellation of assumptions, loyalties, and expectations was undermined. The religious imagination of the Reformers, in other words, 'took no prisoners' and recognised no limits. It threatened to take over not only the realm of the spirit, the intellect and social mores, but to challenge the authority of both church and state. The Word of God itself was frequently described as sword, hammer and fire by the pamphleteers, which if it means anything, means that it has coercive power. Argula von Grumbach quotes Jeremiah 23.29, that God's word is like a hammer smashing rock, immediately after the gentle words of Isaiah 55.10f.; for her, the creativity and menace of the divine Word were quite inseparable.[4] God's Word became judge and lord over all creation. There was a totalitarian threat here to the status quo, not least in its promise for the underdog. Thomas Müntzer styled himself 'Thomas Müntzer, with the hammer'![5]

'The centre cannot hold; Mere anarchy is loosed upon the world', as Yeats put it. What were the results of the Reformation? For many of its contemporaries the answer was *Uffrur*: anarchy, destabilisation, insurrection! Luther himself had warned that, though the Word of God was non-violent, it was the sword of the spirit, and would bring fear, disunity and disruption, *alle aufrur*, upon the godless who resisted it. Christ is described by Spengler as our one true *fechtmeister*, instructor in duelling, an easily misunderstood characterisation.[6]

---

[3]   Balthasar Stanberger, *Ein Epistel oder Sendtbrieff. . . seinem geliebten bruder in Christo Michel Buchfürer . . .* (Erfurt, 1523), quoted Chrisman, *Conflicting Visions*, pp. 120f.

[4]   AvG, pp. 148f.

[5]   CW, p. 260.

[6]   *Spengler Schriften* 1, pp. 386/2; 101/10.

The apocalyptic visions and anticlericalism of the Reformers had upset the clerical apple-cart, but their effects did not stop there. The Reformers repeatedly broached such social problems as self-seeking nobility and princes, money-grubbing merchants and lawyers. When the 'new song' was sung and pulpits rang with praise of the Captain Christ, the worlds of ethics, politics and law were destabilised, especially when we remember that audiences interpreted texts to fit their own circumstances. When verbal violence thumped opponents, who may well have deserved all they got, the passions once released could not be bottled up again. Who could really be surprised that angry words soon shifted to violent actions, given the martyrdom of dear friends? The lure of the imagination slipped all too quickly into the lash of coercion, as frustration and anger built up. How long could people stand by and permit the cynical blocking of desperately needed reforms? As Gordon Rupp has pungently put it: 'History is the lynch law of the universe.'[7] Thwarted dreams generated recidivist nightmares. The era of the Reformation was soon to give way to the era of religious wars.

The very luxuriance of the Reformers' visions became a problem. Interpretations and initiatives varied from place to place, from interest group to interest group. In a phrase that seems to anticipate the Enlightenment, Karlstadt declared: 'I doubt, therefore I ask.'[8] There were too many doubters, too many askers, too many controversies. The foot-folk generally hated this, of course, finding it dire that their leaders were at odds; such tugs at their loyalties confused and worried them. Hieronymus von Endorf noted that 'Even Father Martin has had one follower (Karlstadt) grow into a carbuncle'.[9]

Perhaps there was too much imagination. Under the cruel pressures of time, limited resources, personality conflicts and

---

[7]   *Wisdom and Wit*, p. 7.

[8]   He put it in the mouth of the literary champion of his unorthodox views on the Lord's Supper. *The Essential Carlstadt*, p. 275.

[9]   *Axiomata oder sitig begerungen*, 1525 fol. Aii, quoted Chrisman, *Conflicting Visions*, p. 92.

repression, the less stable figures drifted towards fantasy and harboured messianic illusions that they were the new Daniel come to judgement, the new John the Baptist. We should be cautious, however, about psychologising the issues. The conflicts of interest and the collisions of imagination were as real as the personal failings of all kinds.

To begin with, the repressive, condemnatory tone set by Rome almost guaranteed a nightmarish scenario. It is a falsely understood ecumenism which would seek to pussyfoot around the sinful intransigence of the Curia and most of the German hierarchy. With few exceptions the theological, moral and pastoral challenges posed in the initial years of the Reformation were not attended to; the power question was given priority over the truth question. This failure of moral imagination had tragic consequences. The few exceptions who sought to bridge the chasm, such as Erasmus, Gropper and Contarini, only proved the rule. As Hugo Marschalck put it, reason was banned and public discussion outlawed. It appeared that everything was to be resolved by bans, bulls, and force.[10] Coercion was dignified with a pious mask.

The conflicts between the Reformers were quick to follow. The regional differences, the disagreements about tactics and strategies and priorities were hardly surprising. What was nightmarish was the rapidity with which what may appear to us legitimate differences in doctrine were categorised as perversions of the substance of the faith. Theological road-rage developed as alternative readings of Scripture jostled for the upper hand. Apocalyptic perspectives may be essential to the underdog, but for those in the driving seat they can have fatal consequences.

I have traced elsewhere the 'down-side' to such polemic: the neglect of patience and mutual respect, the despair of reason, the growing blindness to inconvenient facts.[11] Abuse and exaggeration

---

[10] *Von der weyt erschollen Namen Luthers . . .* (Strasbourg, 1523), Aii–Aiiv, quoted Chrisman, *Conflicting Visions*, p. 114.

[11] Matheson, *The Rhetoric of the Reformation*, esp. ch. 7.

became a convenient substitute for *Sachlichkeit*, seeing things as they were. Certainly, the 'devil count' in contemporary pamphlets became formidable. Like the night-flying witches, Satan was sensed to be abroad everywhere, seeking whom he might devour. At Allstedt Luther talked of his erstwhile disciple Müntzer as the devil or Satan, the living incarnation of evil; while Karlstadt seemed to imagine he had swallowed the Holy Ghost, feathers and all.[12] Zwingli and his Swiss and South German followers were labelled 'Sacramentarians', possessed by another spirit.

In turn Luther was denounced by his opponents as the 'new Pope', Dr Liar, the soft-living Flesh in Wittenberg.[13] Such clashes between strong personalities were accentuated by the struggle to find criteria for decision-making, and the structural problem caused by the sin-binning of the traditional arbiters, pope or councils.

Packull makes the point that the frequent schisms between Anabaptists often had little to do with doctrinal or organisational issues. People simply clustered around a person whom they trusted, against those they distrusted.[14] This is certainly correct. At the same time, however, this was a passionately confessional age, agog for the truth with a capital T. As a result, leaders found themselves isolated and elevated, and inclined to arrogate to themselves Mosaic status. Imagine trying to be a non-directive counsellor to Luther or John Eck!

All these factors combined, with dizzying rapidity, to foster an ominous dissonance between the confessional certainties of the age and the empirical reality of doctrinal pluralism. Since the message of Scripture was supposed to be clear, differing interpretations of it were attributed to the deliberate malice and obtuseness of opponents. A classical example of this is the highly public quarrel between Erasmus and Luther about the freedom of the will in 1525, a nightmare to the countless thousands who

---

[12]   LW 40, p. 83.
[13]   CW, pp. 327–8.
[14]   *Hutterite Beginnings*, p. 234 and passim.

regarded them as allies and passionately wanted them to continue as such. Both deserted their natural, imaginative style for clumsy rationalising arguments. They had become gladiators.

The acerbity with which previous allies, mentors, or supporters were assailed may not have been unrelated to the adulation in which they had previously been held. It was Luther, the most monkish of monks, the most loyal son of the Church, who came to regard the pope as none other than Antichrist. As late as 1522 Karlstadt, who was soon to be engaged in bitter polemic with Luther, wrote that Christ had been reborn through Martin; he spoke not only of 'Scripture alone', *sola Scriptura*, but of *solus martinus, dux vitae*: Martin alone, the guide to life![15] The huge effort required to wrench themselves free of their previous loyalties may be visible in the vehemence of the subsequent abuse.

Recent analyses of apocalyptic or millennialist expectations suggest that when an expected transformation fails to transpire, cognitive dissonance sets in. People have to accommodate themselves to a reality that is not as it should be, and the pain can be intolerable. 'I will go on because there is nothing else to do but I feel an emptiness', says the hero Matty in William Golding's *Darkness Visible* when the Last Judgement fails to happen.[16] Everything seems to have gone awry. Their personal and social landscape becomes littered with literal and metaphorical corpses. Doctrinal differences then became nightmares, life and death issues on which no quarter can be given. The *status confessionis*, the very essence of the faith, is believed to be at stake. There is a tendency, in addition, to project on to the opponent the blame for the collapse of one's dreams.

Thus an epidemic of confessionality can be one way of dealing with such massive disappointments. We compensate for the loss of universal acceptance of views by energetically patrolling our own little intellectual and moral frontiers. The imagination seizes up as these are fixed in place. Possibilities for dialogue are lost,

[15]   *The Essential Carlstadt*, p. 132.
[16]   London and Boston: Faber & Faber, 1980, p. 90.

alliances that might have been forged fall by the wayside, the half-open windows of opportunity for women clatter shut again, the brief burgeoning of a communal reformation dies away. The *Annus Mirabilis* of 1520 is overtaken by the *Annus Horribilis* of 1525.

A nightmare, of course, is in the mind. For some it was the dreams themselves which constituted the nightmare. Luther declared repeatedly that he had no time for dreams and dreamers.[17] Everything we needed to know was already there in the Word of God. The very term *Schwärmer*, fantasisers, dreamers, which was cast in the teeth of radicals such as Karlstadt, Müntzer and the Anabaptists, indicates this repugnance for revelations which went beyond Scripture. On a purely theological level this is under-standable, though most would now recognise that Luther operated with a canon within the canon. He controlled his theology by Scripture. But he also read Scripture through a very specific theological lens.

But there is a wider problem. To a much greater degree than he realised, Luther's vision for church and society drew on non-scriptural sources. Like countless contemporaries, he assumed a graded, hierarchical society of princes and subjects, masters and servants, fathers and children, husbands and wives. He took it for granted that this was the God-given order of things. Any attack on it was one on God's good will for creation.[18] This comple-mented his belief in the two realms, his conviction that it would be naive to believe that the values of the Sermon on the Mount could be applied directly to the nitty-gritty world of politics and

---

[17]   Melanchthon was much more open to the suggestiveness of dreams; cf. Siegfried Bräuer: 'Einige aber sind Natürliche, andere Göttliche, wieder andere Teuflische', in *'Man weiss so wenig über ihn'. Philipp Melanchthon. Ein Mensch zwischen Angst und Zuversicht* (ed. Evangelisches Predigerseminar Lutherstadt; Wittenberg: Drei Kastanien Verlag, 1997), pp. 69–99.

[18]   Ironically, for his conception of the relationship between patriarchal family, prince, and cleric he leant heavily on Aristotle, so radically rejected for the understanding of salvation.

the horse-trading of secular life. Indeed, to confuse the world ruled by Gospel and love and that ruled by Law and coercion was a recipe for ecclesiastical and political chaos.

All this is well known. What is less well appreciated is that Luther's central insight that salvation is by grace alone leaked into his 'grace and favour' view of society, of prince and paterfamilias. The dreams of peasants that serfdom could be abolished, the hopes of artisans that they could participate in the running of their community, the conviction of women that, since there was one and the same Christ for both men and women, they too should be encouraged to write and sing and preach: all these conflicted with his 'grace and favour' perspective on society. He had toppled a hierarchical universe in the Church but still hoped to retain intact the layered deferences and structures of the secular universe.[19]

With convenient hindsight it is easy for us to see that, like the vast majority of contemporary opinion-makers, Luther assumed too glibly the alliance of Reformation Gospel with the magisterial authorities. It was, after all, the age of state-building, of early capitalism. The alliance with the magistracy was essential to safeguard the future of Protestantism, as the examples of Poland and Italy demonstrate, though of necessity it brought with it a drawing of prophetic teeth. It is idle to blame him for this, or to apply too quickly the convenient label 'patriarchal'. What was missing was a cool analysis, or perhaps a passionate one, certainly an imaginative one, of such dreams of social liberation.[20] At whose expense were they to be realised? What, if any, was their theological

[19]   The remarkable extent to which Luther maintained outdated models for interpreting society is vividly protrayed in Luise Schorn-Schütte, 'Die Drei-Stände Lehre im reformatorischen Umbruch', *Die frühe Reformation in Deutschland als Umbruch*, pp. 435–61.

[20]   Zorzin has recently pointed out that the Wittenberg presses, compared with those of Augsburg, produced very few pamphlets dealing with peasant issues, and extraordinarily few of the popular Reformation dialogues. Alejandro Zorzin, 'Einige Beobachtungen zu den zwischen 1518 und 1526 im deutschen Sprachbereich veröffentlichten Dialogflugschriften', *Archiv für Reformationsgeschichte* 88 (1997), pp. 77–117, esp. 91f.

justification? Luther did not engage with such issues. He regarded Müntzer, for example, primarily in a political perspective. Luther's advocacy of freedom and Müntzer's championing of liberation were never allowed to be 'thought together', integrated.[21]

We have looked at some of the images of hope which stoked the fires of the Reformation: light, the new dawn, freedom, the living Word of God. But images of terror also stalked the sixteenth-century mind, not unlike the masks of death, plague, or the Turk which people donned at the Lenten carnivals.[22] The impression given by the pamphlets, the sermons, the woodcuts and the popular songs is that these images lurked just under the surface, a subterranean repertoire of horror always ready to burst up to the surface.

There was the nightmare of sexual depravity. Rome has become a brothel, convents are brothels and murder-pits, the Reformers proclaim. Müntzer has the godless slithering like snakes into their lust, forging the unforgettable image of the collaboration of rulers and clerics as a writhing mass of eels and snakes all copulating together.[23] There is the very familiar but recurrent association of the papacy with the whore of Babylon and other sexual deviations or, rather, obsessions. Less well known are the obscene fantasies of the celibate devotees of the Virgin Mary about any evangelical women who dared to challenge her role as queen of heaven.[24] The witch-craze is a particularly pathological form of this fear: sexuality as a master image of all depravity. There was the nightmarish vision of Germany as a den of thieves, another Jeremiah image.[25] Woodcuts remind us that at many a crossroad the distorted bodies of robbers hung, sometimes a whole gang of them, sprawled in

[21]   Matheson, 'The Cornflower in the Wheatfield'.

[22]   One of the best sources of these images of depravity, lust, robbery, inversion of the truth, blindness, monstrosity, etc. is Meuche's edition of the *Flugblätter der Reformation*.

[23]   CW, pp. 244f.

[24]   Cf. the attacks of Georg Hauer and 'Johannes of Landshut' on Argula von Grumbach; AvG, pp. 19f., 166f.

[25]   Jeremiah 7.

Lucas Cranach, the Older. Illustration for New Testament of 1522,
Revelation 17

the agony of death. People lived with such ghastly sights. To princes, magistrates, merchants and university teachers nothing was so alarming as the omnipresent threat to their sacred property rights, especially if it were legitimated by an appeal to Scripture. The Anabaptists might insist that when they spoke of sharing goods they were talking about a voluntary communism, not a forcible take-over. After the Peasants' War, however, no one was prepared to listen. The dream of *omnia sunt communa*, all things being held in common, galvanised the forces of repression as nothing else could have.

On the other hand the rage of those who for the first time had the opportunity to read Genesis 1 and Acts 2 in their own language knew no bounds, as they compared the 'order of creation' they saw depicted there with the realities of contemporary oppression, with new-fangled laws depriving them of access to rivers to fish, woods to hunt and pastures to graze the cattle.

> Open your eyes! What is the evil brew from which all usury, theft and robbery springs but the assumption of our lords and princes that . . . the fish in the water, the birds in the air, the plants on the face of the earth – it all has to belong to them . . . While they do violence to everyone, flay and fleece the poor . . . yet should any of the latter commit the pettiest crime, he must hang. And Doctor Liar says, Amen.[26]

One of the most passionate denunciations of the tyranny, robbery and arbitrary violence of both 'empires', those of the pope and the emperor (who stand for all the ruling classes), is Johannes Locher's *Second Letter to Karsthans from the Peasants' Enemy*. It notes that the only 'writing' with which the 'empires' communicate with the peasants is violence, fire and the sword, and culminates with the apocalyptic warning: 'Things simply cannot go on like this; the game has run its course, and the towns as well as the peasants will tolerate it no more.'[27]

---

[26] CW, p. 335.
[27] *Flugschriften der Bauernkriegszeit* (ed. Adolf Laube, etc.; Berlin: Akademie Verlag, 1975), pp. 102/10f., 107/12ff. (my translation).

Woodcuts got across the message that the 'bigwigs', the rich and the powerful, got away with 'murder' time and time again. And their theft was not only of temporal wealth but also of cultural and spiritual wealth. Lay people were barred from access to Scripture and books in their own language, and were fobbed off with trite catechism verities. The priests had stolen the key of Scripture, locking it up. Just as the storks vomited up pre-digested hunks of food to their young, the clergy and the scholars patronised the ordinary person.[28] Real knowledge was reserved for the élite. The nightmare vision of Germany as a den of thieves was as real for the oppressed as for those in positions of power. The tyrannous rulers of church and state preyed on the poor like Nimrod the mighty hunter; they snared the innocent, butchered them like meat on a chopping-block, devoured them, flayed them alive.[29] Ulrich von Hutten is one of many who uses the cannibalistic motif. The pope and his followers had become like a monstrous caterpillar, devouring the flesh and sucking away the life-blood of the German people.[30] The images of sexual depravity are frequently combined with those of oppression. In South Tyrol the seventeen-year-old Katharina Tagwericher denounced the churches as 'damned temples of idols, whore-houses and murderers' dens'.[31]

Then there was the terror of pollution, of disease, filth and poison. As cancer stalks our minds today, the plague haunted people then. Virtually every family had lost relatives to it; everyone had memories of the utter terror it provoked. The revived attention to the purity laws of the Pentateuch may also have sharpened the fear of a moral and spiritual pollution, a fast-spreading plague

---

[28]   CW, p. 365.
[29]   LW 36, p. 12; CW, p. 43, n. 273; CW, p. 95; innumerable pamphlets speak of *schinden und schaben*, the flaying of the poor.
[30]   *Hutten, Müntzer, Luther. Werke in zwei Bänden* (ed. Siegfried Streller; Berlin Weimar, 1982), p. 140; quoted by Hans-Jürgen Goertz, *Thomas Müntzer Apocalyptic Mystic and Revolutionary* (tr. Jocelyn Jaquiery; Edinburgh, 1993).
[31]   Packull, *Hutterite Beginnings*, p. 173.

which would forfeit one's salvation for all eternity. To condone heresy in others was to defile oneself, to provoke God's wrath on the entire community. Censorship of books and pamphlets, measures against authors, booksellers and readers flowed from such antiseptic concerns.

Closely associated with the fear of heresy was that of blasphemy. Even those who realised the folly of trying to impose their theological views on others, even those with a profound understanding of the inviolability of the individual conscience, could have no truck with blasphemy. It was an honour-laden culture, and to deprive God of honour was to invite disaster on everyone.

Anabaptists who mocked the host as a piece of baked dough, Protestants who refused to make the sign of the cross before the Virgin, Jews who rejected Christ as Messiah, could expect no mercy. Burn their blasphemous synagogues down, drive them out!

Thus sexual 'deviants', thieves, polluters, idolators were all seen as masked agents of Satan. Behind them all, however, and most incomprehensibly to us, there loomed the terrifying apocalyptic image of Anti-Christ, often associated with the papacy, the bodily incarnation of evil as Luther saw it. In his late tract, *The Papacy at Rome, Founded by the Devil*, he developed his views most fully.[32] It is almost unreadable today and I will not tarry on it here because I have dealt with it elsewhere.[33] We do well, however, not to sweep it aside as the ravings of an old and sick man. This is apocalyptic analysis, drawn from a nightmarish vision of evil. If we recoil at its sadistic, anal and obscene language, that is, in part, precisely what we were intended to do. When the reality is gross, language should be gross too, Luther believed.

The grotesque and monstrous images with which Cranach and others depict the papacy remind us that contemporaries believed that the skylights of the heavens, so to speak, had been opened up. It was as if the detritus from the cosmic battle was continually

[32]   LW 41, pp. 263–376.
[33]   *The Rhetoric of the Reformation*, pp. 199–214.

Erhard Schön, c. 1535. Devil with Bagpipes, *Flugblätter, Nr. 16*

being jettisoned on to the earthly scene. Satan, contemporaries believed, had been stirred to unparalleled fury by the moral, educational, liturgical and doctrinal initiatives of the Reformation. There was a broad consensus that in the history of salvation the extremes of good and evil always coincided. While angels sang to the newborn babe, Herod's thugs gathered to slaughter the innocent.[34] A tradition stretching right back to the early Church held that Satan's most dangerous strategy to subvert the Church was not outward persecution, but heresy and schism from within.[35] The devil was accordingly spotted, identified and localised in religious opponents from Rome to Strasbourg to Wittenberg: in monks, judaisers, spiritualisers, witches and rebaptisers. Erhard Schön's devastating image of the monk as, quite literally, an organ of the devil is an unforgettable example of this.[36]

The model for people's thinking was that of possession. One was either possessed by Christ or the devil, there was no middle way. The flip-side, then, to the elation at the breakthrough to a new reading of the Gospel was abysmal despair when this reading was challenged by a succession of radically different ones or even, to our eyes at least, by marginally different ones. For they threatened to undermine all that had been achieved. When this happened the archetypal visions of depravity, theft, murder, heresy, blasphemy and Anti-Christ surfaced in the popular imagination. The masks were off. Evil strutted its stuff for all to see. The pervasive image of the monstrous monk-calf, immortalised by Cranach, catches the conviction that the core of reality had been perverted, the genetic stock of creation, as it were, distorted. Monstrosities walked the earth.[37]

The nightmare scenario took many forms, and we may under-estimate the grit it must have required to resist total despair. Erasmus, representative of the urbanity of the humanists, their

---

[34]   CW, pp. 281–3.

[35]   This theme is developed by Luther at the beginning of his *Brief an die Fürsten zu Sachsen von dem aufrührischen Geist*, WA 15, 210ff., but it is also a favourite topic of Müntzer: 'When the Lord introduces the preaching of the Gospel of the kingdom throughout the world then the abomination of desolation is revealed.' CW, p. 35.

[36]   'Der Teufel mit der Sackpfeife', *c.* 1535; *Flugblätter der Reformation*, Nr. 16.

[37]   *Flugblätter der Reformation*, Nrs 37, 50.

Unknown Artist, 1522. Monstrous Calf, *Flugblätter, Nr. 37*

hopes for a new age of civility, and humane, mediatory language, found himself vilified on all sides by the end of his life. Erasmians in Spain and Italy were tarred with a Lutheran brush. The Church he loved was split by ferocious polemic. The campaign for a biblical humanism open to lay people, for a reformed Catholicism, appeared to be a casualty of an escalating series of apocalyptic confrontations.

The loss of Christian unity was for many the worst nightmare of all. Many Catholic observers spoke of the ruin of all religion. It was as if Zion itself had been sacked, devastated, levelled to the ground. For reforming Catholics such as Erasmus, the Temple of Jerusalem, drawing all nations to it, where even the sparrow could find its rest, had been a controlling image of harmony and beauty and peace. A church that was not united simply was no longer the Church. The Eucharist, the symbol of unity, had become the fulcrum of divisiveness. The seamless robe of Christ, another favoured image, had been rent apart. Even the thugs around the cross had not fallen as low as that.

Towards the end of his life, therefore, Erasmus found himself stressing increasingly the need for the authority of the Church and the myths of continuity. The élitist elements in the humanist approach shouldered out its more inclusive tendencies. The extraordinarily crude polemic of the older Sir Thomas More against the Reformers was another mirror of such interior nightmares.

Then there was the tragedy of the Imperial Knights, whose genuine evangelicalism was overlaid by a swashbuckling pursuit of anachronistic freedoms and greed for church land. The Knights' War of 1523–4 had its pale shadows later on, not least under Wilhelm von Grumbach in Franconia, but effectively it was their last fling. Custer's last stand! Many died heroically defending their obsolescent castles, but it is a telling point that one of their most effective adversaries was the future Protestant leader and close ally of Martin Bucer, Philip of Hesse.

Another nightmare was that of the guildsmen, and certainly the lesser artisans, who found themselves in city after city out-manoeuvred by the patrician authorities, who settled for allies among the princes. Some of the lesser guilds had made common cause with the rebellious peasants in 1525 and were fired with the same enthusiasm for a theology of creation based on Genesis 1, a democratised republic and a participatory Church.

This raises the larger issue of lay influence and the deep anxiety the demand for it had provoked. Luther's *Appeal to the German Nobility* had 'reinvented' the Church on the basis of baptism. All were to be priests and kings, not only individually but corporately as well. Karlstadt insisted that a Christian congregation was not passive but active and participatory, poised to exercise righteousness; it had ears to hear, eyes to see. In some of his pamphlets he described himself, professor and theologian, as a new lay person.[38] He dressed in peasant garb. Peasant spokesmen such as Karsthans, waving his flail like Christ cleansing the Temple, cobblers like Hans Sachs and prophetic women such as Argula von Grumbach seemed to be heralds of a new era. Christ had, after all, chosen the unlearned to be his disciples and walked amongst whores, publicans and the despised, as Thomas Stör pointed out.[39] Lay people could no longer be condemned unheard and unread simply because they were not clerics. In one reformation dialogue after another, peasant spokesmen had all the good lines.

Thus many lay people lost their traditional deference for both church and political leaders. Such egalitarianism deeply concerned Luther, who insisted on a variety of roles, reinstituted the standing of the preacher and, interestingly, criticised a quest for authenticity which sought to dispense with all masks: the Church always appears masked or costumed. 'Such masks are a husband, a ruler, a servant, John, Peter, Luther, Amsdorf; and yet the church is none of these, for the church is neither Jew nor Greek.'[40] Significantly, some of the fiercest repression was against lay artists such as Jörg Ratgeb or the three 'godless painters' in Nuremberg, the Behaim brothers and Georg Pencz, who were accused of displaying a stiff-necked lack of respect both for the pastors and the magistrates; lay insubordination was spilling out into the secular sphere.[41] During the Peasants' War itself lay people began

---

[38]   *The Essential Carlstadt*, pp. 253, 185.
[39]   *Von dem christlichen Weingarten . . .* , Aiir, Fiche 99/261.
[40]   W Br. 9, p. 610/47ff.
[41]   *Reformation in Nürnberg*, pp. 173f.

to claim not only the right to appoint their pastors but also the power of the keys, the right to exercise forgiveness, and the right, in the ring, to exercise people's justice, the right to legislate.

The real crime of the peasants, then, was not their disorderliness but their alarming propensity to create a new egalitarian order. Since 1975 scholarship has been clarifying that the campaigns of the Peasants' War were remarkably disciplined, organised and focused.[42] They spared the crops and respected the parish churches, destroying only the oppressive abbeys, nunneries and castles. If the peasant armies had possessed some cavalry and more artillery they might well have prevailed. The real nightmare for the defenders of the social order was not the peasants' casual violence or plundering, but that they developed their own chancelleries and social programmes, and that they championed an alternative vision of the *ordo rerum*, the divine order. Their preachers told them that God would not tolerate the injustice they suffered. They had a good conscience about their actions. They were, despite Thomas Müntzer's criticism of their 'self-seeking' on the eve of his death, probably as religiously motivated as any group in the sixteenth century.[43] 'This Christian Union and alliance has been founded to the praise and honor of Almighty God, invoking the holy Gospel and Word of God, also to assist justice and godly laws.' There are innumerable calls in their articles to trust in God, to let the truth blossom in this new age of grace, with references to Luke 19 and similar passages – Christ driving the money-lenders out of the Father's house.[44]

But why did their apocalyptic, biblical, and anticlerical reading of reality clash with that of Luther and the Protestant as well as the Catholic princes? Miriam Chrisman argues that the preaching

---

[42]   Cf. the introduction to Scott and Scribner, *The German Peasants' War*, pp. 1–64, and the review of historiography in Stayer, *The German Peasants' War*, pp. 19–44.

[43]   'they sought only their own interests and the divine truth was defeated as a result'. CW, p. 160.

[44]   Scott and Scribner, *The German Peasants' War*, p. 130.

of the reforming Gospel had in fact set off a whole series of revolutions. The reforms which continued after 1525 'were only half of the Reform envisioned by lower ranks. Their deep longing for control of their own religious life and for fundamental social change was repressed. The message of the Gospel had been tamed by the powerful.' [45]

The mayor of Zwickau wrote on 4 June 1525 to a friend. Why, he asked, had Luther become the 'hammer of the poor'? He deplored the violence with which the nobility imposed burdens on the people with the sword and shed the blood of the suffering poor. Why was the middle way ignored, why had there been no meaningful negotiations? As there had been at Strasbourg or Würzburg and Heilbronn, he might have added, where the men and, above all, the women of the city insisted on it?[46]

Certainly the dimensions of this particular tragedy were huge. It has been computed that some 100,000 people died in the Peasants' War, the men strung up like crows on the trees, the women ravaged and left to die in ditches, the children left hungry and desolate in that terrible winter of 1525–6. We have become sated with holocausts in our own century and may be unimpressed by these statistics, but behind them lie extraordinary stories of resistance, courage and insight, as well as of heartbreak and broken lives. For many the war seemed to combine all the features of previous nightmares: immorality, robbery, blasphemy, anarchy.

And who was to blame? A fine crop of popular songs appeared shortly after the war. Some are the vindictive rants one would expect: peasants who had forgotten their oaths of loyalty and imbibed deep draughts of courage from barrels of wine had got the come-uppance they deserved. They had wanted to share everything in common; for all their prattling about the Gospel, obviously their real God was to be found in the money chests they raided. They had got totally out of their depth. Their chief fault was their *übermut* – literally, their excess courage. And now after

---

[45]   Chrisman, *Conflicting Visions*, p. 229.
[46]   Scott and Scribner, *The German Peasants' War*, pp. 322–4.

defeat they pretended, of course, that they had never been involved at all. They had reached too high, got above themselves:

> Bauren mit grossen herren
> die söllen spilen nit.
> Peasants meet disaster
> When they play games with their masters.[47]

This was the greatest nightmare of all for contemporaries: *keiner sich helt nach seinem stand*; no one kept to their place in society, with anarchy as a result, *uffrur*, the collapse of all law and order. Unless the proper distinctions were maintained between the different estates in society, there could never be any stability or harmony. The peasants had transgressed against their oaths of loyalty to their betters, they had transgressed the world order established by God and could not expect to escape punishment.[48]

Another contemporary folk song, from an evangelical perspective, suggests that the peasants began with good intentions but were led astray by the wealth of the Old Church clergy to grab for wealth themselves

> At which the Devil laughed
> And set the merry game in train . . .

The clergy had tricked the authorities into believing they would be next on the line if they allowed the clergy to be attacked. If only the Word of God had been preached, none of this would have happened. The Catholics believe they have won, but like Christ the truth will only remain buried a short time.

> Though some have abused it
> The word itself stays true
> Though wine makes the drunkard stagger
> The wine itself is pure
> Gold stays pure and good
> However oft abused . . .[49]

---

[47]   Liliencron 3, Nr. 375, p. 446; Nr. 387, p. 497; Nr. 398, p. 500.
[48]   Liliencron 3, Nr. 37, p. 464.
[49]   Liliencron 3, Nr. 393, pp. 510–12.

Slowly, painfully, we may have to learn to read the dreams and nightmares of the Reformation together. Until the nightmare is squarely faced we shall not do justice to the dream. We have to question some of the labelling of nightmare. We are beginning to recognise that the Peasants' War was no total failure. Many of the demands it made were quietly conceded in its aftermath. We cannot talk of people being totally cowed. Countless other revolts were to follow. Hut and his Anabaptist followers continued to dream of vengeance. The radical printer, Hans Hergot, in 1526 produced *On the Transformation of the Christian Life*, calling Luther to account for his cruel attacks on the peasants, and in the spirit of Müntzer predicting a new age of the Spirit in which everything would be held in common by the members of 'God's house'. No one would say any more 'This is mine'. All would eat out of the one bowl. The Lord's Prayer, in which we speak of 'Our' Father, would become reality. Faith and life would be one.[50]

Münster in 1534–5, for example, harboured a genuine experiment in communal reformation, the provision of a city of refuge for the oppressed, in egalitarianism and a church based on adult baptism. What Stayer calls its tawdry war communism was only the last phase.[51] Tyrolean Anabaptism, as Lassmann and Packull have suggested, had genuine communal support, fired by hatred of Austrian oppression. The dangerous memory of the people lingered on in Anabaptism and, as Oberman has reminded us, in the Reformed tradition.

This was a era committed to the quest for a new order, *ein christliche frydsame ordnung zu machen*, as the peasant radical Johannes Locher called it.[52] Convinced that a rediscovered Scripture pointed the way, impressive numbers of people were ready to speak out whatever the cost and to die for it, like the

[50]   *Von der neuen Wandlung eines christlichen Lebens*, pp. 548/4ff.; 549/9f.
[51]   Stayer, *The German Peasants' War*, pp. 123–38.
[52]   Locher, *Ein Sendbrief an Karsthans (Flugschriften der Bauernkriegszeit)*, p. 966.

artist Jörg Ratgeb, whose Pasolini-like depictions of Christ and his followers have been referred to above. His bestial execution for high treason, torn apart by horses, like Jacob Hutter's still more sadistic end, provides indirect testimony to the effectiveness of his message.

As historians we have a duty to honour the memory of the dreamers, to note that the dreams of some become the nightmares of others, and to take care that we do not perpetuate injustice by adopting uncritically the terminology of the oppressor. From a theological perspective it may be true that all are oppressors and all oppressed, but we do well to be cautious that this is not said too glibly and prematurely. From a political perspective we may have to ask about effective strategies for liberation, including what the Germans call *Sachlichkeit*, keeping one's feet on the ground;[53] from a church perspective, about the need to provide sanctuary and mediation. And, as we will see in the final two chapters, there are individual and spiritual perspectives as well.

---

[53]   A sober and helpful reflection on this in Andrew Bradstock, *Faith in the Revolution. The Political theologies of Müntzer and Winstanley* (London: SPCK, 1997).

CHAPTER FIVE

THE CONTOURS OF DAILY LIFE

Whether we speak analytically or in more personal terms about family life, we tend to assume a certain geography of human relationships, what we take to constitute the civilised contours of daily intercourse. More than we realise, however, these are social constructs which change from age to age. One generation's happy family is the next's repressive nightmare. The Reformation both mirrored and itself provoked dramatic changes in the way people structured their day, week, year, their patterns of politeness, openness or inhibitedness, the personal space claimed, their rites of passage, even their choice of domestic bric-à-brac. The networks of friends and correspondents, the type of journeys made, the schools attended, the obligations assumed, all these, and more, were transformed by the Reformation. In this area of social relationships much remained the same, yet the role of parents and children, husbands and wives, kith and kin was sometimes abruptly, sometimes subtly, changed. Yesterday's concubine emerged as the evangelical pastor's wife. Celibate communities, the nunneries hallowed by centuries, were dissolved or relegated to slow decay. Work and home came to be celebrated as the true laboratories for godliness.

The Reformation is not only about macro-history, the grand strategies and battles for church and society. We may have to recover what Thierry Wanegffelen has recently called '*l'histoire de la personne croyante*', the religious sensibility of individuals, the level ground of faith, '*le plat pays de la croyance*', as compared with the great mountain ranges of synods, councils, ordinances for church polity and worship.[1] Lucien Febvre has talked memorably of the 'red wine and cheese of history', its passion and colour. What did individuals feel like as part of a disintegrating world, being swept into an emerging one, almost suffocated by nightmare, allured by vision, struggling manfully, womanfully, for survival, with the occasional glimpse of moments of grace?

Perhaps people matter. Perhaps even dead people have a right to our respect. Among those of a literary bent, there seems some danger that these days the human womb in which the text is nurtured will be forgotten. We will be left with the naked, screaming child, the text, or rather abandoned to the tender deconstructing mercies of its interpreters. In the world of cultural studies, it often seems unfashionable to root sources in the mother earth of their contingent circumstance. Some, on the other hand, genuinely believe that they can explain everything in terms of social factors, a sort of 'history without actors' as Alain Peyrefitte has put it.[2] Here context becomes all. Even some of our very best social historians find it difficult to move from their empathetic field-work to the actual presentation of their analysis without cloaking themselves in an ironic distance which, as the best of them are well aware, is in danger of imputing alien motives, beliefs, meanings and even functions to the society they are studying.[3]

On a popular level this can lead us to regard pre-modern, or even pre-post-modern, people as if they were strange animals in a zoo. A recent TV programme offering an 'unauthorised biography

---

[1]   Thierry Wanegffelen, *Ni Rome ni Genève. Des Fidèles entre deux chaires en France au XVIe siécle* (Paris: Honoré Champion, 1997), pp. ix–xx.

[2]   Alain Peyrefitte, *La société de confiance* (Paris, 1995), pp. 312–13.

[3]   Johannes Fabian, *Time and the Other: How Anthropology Makes its Object* (New York: Columbia University Press, 1983), p. 157. I am indebted for this reference to Paul Rorem's inaugural lecture of 25 March 1998, in Princeton Theological Seminary: 'Empathy and Evaluation in Medieval Church History and Pastoral Ministry: A Lutheran Reading of Pseudo-Dionysius', *The Princeton Seminary Bulletin* Vol. XIX, Nr. 2 N.S. (1998), pp. 99–115, which suggests a dialectic of empathetic listening and critical evaluation.

of the Devil' dealt sweepingly with the Inquisition, the persecution
of the Cathari, the Renaissance, the Reformation, the Witch-
hunt and Auschwitz, in forty minutes or so. It was fronted by a
smiling young man who gave the distinct impression that all this
monstrous evil was the invention of the Christians and in
particular of Martin Luther. For this viewer a plethora of images
and sound-bites had supplanted all intelligent analysis. History as
collage.

To understand the Reformation we need to pay attention to
both text and context, but we also need in-depth studies of
particular individuals and families as they sought imaginatively to
restructure their own and their families' lives. Off and on over the
past two years I have been working on the personal papers of a
Bavarian noblewoman, Argula von Grumbach, from 1520–45.
These include shopping lists for the kitchen, bills from tradesmen,
court cases and wills, but also a treasury of private prayers, letters
to friends, creditors and clerics, but above all to her children and
their teachers, and from them to her. Unlike her published letters,
which call courageously for the reformation of church, society
and theology, these are intimate family communications, never
meant for any eyes except her own proud and often anguished
ones. It is a miracle that they have survived. I have wondered about
the ethics of using them.

But her own published material frankly outlines her own
traumas and dreams for a public audience, showing how she
struggled against her own hesitations, and against traditional
church inhibitions on women speaking out, to develop a new
reading of Scripture. She deliberately entered the public square.
One of the main contributions of women writers like her may
well be this willingness to be personal.

Born in 1492 into the aristocratic von Stauff family, Argula
was orphaned as a young teenager and brought up in the glittering
Munich court. Married off to a less than exciting Franconian
nobleman, Frederick von Grumbach, she dutifully produced four
children for him, but was undutifully drawn to the evangelical
views circulating at nearby Würzburg. Despite his opposition, and

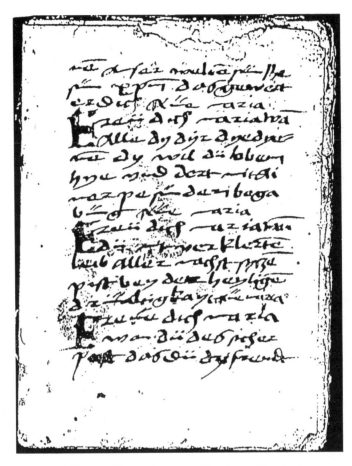

Collection of Prayers in papers of Argula von Grumbach

indeed open hostility, she quietly persevered in them, but then entered the public arena in 1523 with a remarkable challenge to Ingolstadt's startled theologians. They had staged a show trial of a young student, Arsacius Seehofer, for his Lutheran views.

Argula von Grumbach, a lay person, and a woman to boot, challenged them to a public debate based on Scripture. Like her other protests to princes and city councils, this letter was not even acknowledged. For a while it circulated in samizdat copies but was soon published and went through an astonishing fourteen editions. The public interest was extraordinary.

There remains considerable mystery about Argula's life. For a couple of years she lived in the bright blaze of publicity, as one pamphlet after another appeared; but after 1524, apart from an occasional reference in Luther's correspondence, she all but disappeared from public view. If it were not for the accident of her family papers having survived, we would know virtually nothing about her. It reminds us how little documentation has survived, particularly in the case of women. We do not even know for certain when she died, though her name lives on in the little villages in which she spent the rest of her life. There is something very touching about this thin trail of evidence.

German scholars, on the whole, have been remarkably slow to grasp her significance. Indeed, apart from a New Zealander like myself, it has been a liberation theologian in Argentina and a woman professor in Princeton who have been the first to bring out editions of the women theologians of the Reformation.[4]

Why did Argula von Grumbach suddenly cease to write any more pamphlets? Was it connected with the Peasants' War, the threats on her own life, or pressure from her Catholic husband and family? Why in her remaining letters are there so few explicit references to the Reformation's progress, even to personal piety or Scripture?

Working through her papers – the apparent trivia of purchases for estate, kitchen and wardrobe, the problems with unreliable farm managers, the strident pleas from her teenage children for money or clothes or food or visits or letters, the veiled threats from money-lenders – you begin to glimpse the huge iceberg

---

[4] Cf. Elsie Anne McKee, *The Writings of Katharina Schütz Zell*; and *Katharina Schütz Zell: The Life and Thought of a Sixteenth Century Reformer* (Leiden: Brill, 1998); also the forthcoming Spanish edition and translation of women Reformers' writings by Alejandro Zorzin.

usually hidden from sight in conventional Reformation histories: the day-to-day struggles against bankruptcy, the harsh realities of illness, isolation and loneliness.

We need to read her life in the context of the times. Marriage and family figured more prominently in the new evangelical dispensation and may have been expected to carry too many social functions, although relations between men and women, parents and children, continued to be determined largely by communal and kinship interests. The family models which triumphed were often, as Lyndal Roper has shown for Augsburg, patriarchal ones.[5] There were constant tensions between the generations, which flared up on such issues as arranged marriages and inheritance. One of the surprises will be to see how passionately Protestant clergy, from Luther down, supported what we would see as the tyranny of parental and kinship interests over the imperatives of young love, as in the very influential handbook of Justus Menius, (1499–1558), *Oeconomia christiana, das ist von christlicher Haushaltung.*[6]

The days have long since passed when we could speak with confidence if not complacency about the positive models of family life emerging with the Reformation, of humanists and reformers joining hands in an educational crusade. A considerable consensus is developing on the deficits in the educational field (certainly in the short term), in relation to rural communities, and in social and economic opportunities for women. We can no longer take at face value the 'literature of aspiration' produced by the Reformation, its sermons and manuals of conduct.

On the other hand, it may not be helpful to swing to the other extreme. Invaluable as the study of wills, tax records and court cases may be, which tends to be the happy hunting ground of the

[5]   *Holy Household: Women and Morals in Reformation Augsburg* (Oxford: Oxford University Press, 1991).

[6]   Analysed by Luise Schorn-Schütte, 'Die Drei-Stände-Lehre im reformatorischen Umbruch', *Die frühe Reformation in Deutschland als Umbruch*, pp. 442–4.

social historians, it may not take us much closer than sermons to the 'red wine and cheese' of personal history. I shall be leaning in this chapter on the work of Steven Ozment, who has produced a remarkable series of personal histories of individual families, based on private letters and diaries. His 'Intimate Portrait' of the marriage of the Nuremberg couple, Balthasar Paumgartner and Magdalena Behaim, portrays their courtship and marriage in terms of thoughtful partnership and warm affection. Not naturally a lyrical soul, Balthasar hated the separation his work as a merchant forced betweeen him and Magdalena, his 'dearest treasure' (after God, of course), and longed to return 'into our little chamber or flower-garden'.[7] Magdalena, for her part, swooned into his arms when he returned. An apparently solitary angry exchange between them shocked them out of their minds. Magdalena was an impressively organised and compassionate person. She had no truck with the idea that brides should be sidelined in premarital negotiations. The impression is that she quietly manipulated her menfolk, without them having any awareness of it.

Just being a widow made one very vulnerable, as illustrated in the correspondence of Argula von Grumbach with her friend Dorothea von Klingen, whose life was devastated by the ruthless greed and violence of her male relatives, despite Argula's attempts to support her.[8] Argula herself had to cope with the refusal of rents due to her, with difficult relatives and, in 1541, with the petition against her to the Bavarian dukes of one of her subjects, Sebastian Stockl. He had occupied a house he was not entitled to

<hr />

[7]   Steven Ozment, *Magdalena and Balthasar. An Intimate Portrait of Life in 16th century Europe Revealed in the Letters of a Nuremberg Husband and Wife* . . . (New York: Simon & Schuster, 1986), p. 40; cf. also the same author's *When Fathers Ruled. Family Life in Reformation Europe* (Harvard University Press, 1983); *Three Behaim Boys. Growing up in Early Modern Germany* (New Haven and London: Yale University Press, 1990).

[8]   On Argula von Grumbach, cf. Silke Halbach, *Argula von Grumbach als Verfasserin reformatorischer Flugschriften* (Europäische Hochschulschriften. Series XXIII Theology: Vol. 468; Frankfurt am Main, 1992); Personenselekt Cat. 110 (Grombach) Bayerische Haupstaatsarchiv, Munich.

and threatened and insulted her, or so she said; so she put him in the stocks. He had been in prison and whipped in Ingolstadt before, and involved in the Peasants' Revolt; he denied all these accusations.[9] She also bitterly resisted the attempts of the Ingolstadt judge, Sigmund Nuremberger, to obtain insight into her financial affairs in order to exercise guardianship over her children in 1542, as she had previously resisted the attempts of the noblemen appointed as her children's guardians.[10]

This, we recognise, is life as it is lived in reality. We enter the unremittingly hard shadow side of the religious imagination of the Reformers. Perhaps, as we do so, we may be able to empathise better and see the human face of the Reformation. For the great plans for the reform of church and society, as outlined in her pamphlets, had fallen on deaf ears. Argula von Grumbach had failed to influence the princes, the university or the city councils. Loyalty to the papacy, the hierarchy, the traditional understanding of the sacraments, remained unshaken. Scripture did not win out as the sole norm for life and doctrine. Indeed, Ingolstadt became a theological centre of the emergent Counter-Reformation and the Bavarian dukes became key players in the forging of a Catholic resistance.

This was cognitive dissonance with a vengeance! Remarkably, however, Argula managed to keep the apocalyptic flag flying and to move beyond anticlericalism to constructive action. She patiently built up the structures of a new life in miniature, around her family, her circle of friends, her little estates, wherever she had leverage in the local context, both in Bavaria and Franconia. She was able not only to maintain her own faith, but to find, within the interstices of a Catholic society, space to foster evangelical worship and life.

She did this by developing networks of support among her own family, her husbands' families and a variety of male and

---

[9]   Ibid.
[10]   Ibid.

female friends, only some of whom are known to us.[11] The city clerk in Catholic Würzburg, Martin Cronthal, for example, speaks of her as his 'dear sister in Christ' and acts on her behalf in relation to property issues such as the proper supervision of her vineyards; there are clearly warm connections between her and his wife; Cronthal sends on to her a letter from Luther; we hear of pamphlets that they have been exchanging.[12] It would be fascinating to know more about this particular correspondence. She had a friendship with the Reformer of Nuremberg, Osiander, and corresponded with many of the Wittenberg Reformers, including Spalatin and Luther himself. She was in touch with various evangelical families, offering and receiving mutual consolation and comfort at times of illness and bereavement; even her relationship to one of the Jewish money-lenders was not a purely professional one – she knew his wife and family, too, and greeted them. Unfortunately, few of her letters to her relatives have survived.

The adoption of evangelical views could, of course, split households, as happened in Argula's own case; her husband and many of his relatives remained true to Catholicism. Indeed, he lost his well-paid position as the castellan at Dietfurt because of her, which cannot have increased his sympathy for the Lutheran cause. Her brother Bernhardin, although far from a good exemplar of the reforming cause, had his wife Otilie leave him, at least in part because of his new beliefs.[13] Clearly Argula von Grumbach must have had to make many compromises. She seems to have retained the affection of those who took a different path from her.

---

[11]   There are, for example, no letters in her correspondence from Osiander, the leading Nuremberg Reformer, who we know was her confidant and adviser, and none from Reformers such as Paul Speratus, Balthasar Hubmaier, Johann Eberlin von Günzburg, not to mention Melanchthon, Karlstadt, Luther himself, although we have published letters of Luther referring to correspondence with her.

[12]   Personenselekt Cat. 110 (Grombach).

[13]   Ibid.

All her children, however, followed her in the evangelical faith, as did many of her own family and even her husband's family.

She procured Lutheran pamphlets from Wittenberg and elsewhere, and distributed them to others. She seems to have taught and preached herself. She brought pressure on the local preacher, Jacob, in her property at Zeilitzhaim, to preach the Word of God. Even today the local tradition in the little village of Zeilitzhaim attributes to her the founding of the Lutheran church which still stands there.

Argula corresponded with liberal clerics in the Old Church, such as Frederick von Leonrodt, a canon at Eichstätt who saw the need for reform but, in Erasmian style, feared that an impetuous approach would do more harm than good. He responded to a (lost) letter of hers which appears to have emphasised the piety and scholarship of the evangelical representatives at the forthcoming Diet of Augsburg in 1530. 'God grant that they use their gifts well . . . and give them grace to make good the wicked and disgusting things they have done, while . . . reforming the wicked abuses in the spiritual and secular estates.' Argula travelled to Augsburg to lend her support to the Protestant delegates there, and took the chance to visit Luther himself, holed up in the Coburg Castle, apparently giving him a lecture, Dr Spock style, on best current practice for weaning his children. Luther, it seems, was impressed by more than her maternal skills.

Thus she maintained, long after the Peasants' War, her sense of a prophetic calling to speak out at times of crisis. She, a lay woman, urged the Lutheran theologians and leaders at Augsburg not to despair at what was a highly anxious time for them: God who began it all in us, and without us, had everything in hand and would protect us and bring the Diet to a safe conclusion; God, who never slept on the job, was our guardian, our *Beschützer*, she said, referring to Psalm 121.[14]

Argula was a mother of four. It may be salutary to remember that this was a world in which one-third of children died before

---

[14]   As Justas Jonas reports to Luther; W Br. 5, p. 536.

the age of five; 1,600 children are said to have died of small-pox in Nuremberg in one year, 1570. It was a world before pain-killers and antibiotics, reliant on herbs and house books, and family and oral tradition, and now without the hope that saints, relics, pilgrimages or the sacraments would protect and heal. Again, we cannot attribute this change solely to Protestantism. Pre-Reformation manuals on child birth, such as the *Rosengarten*, tended to be purely practical, with no reference to St Margaret.[15]

Illness could be unbelievably grim. Magdalena Behaim writes of the slow death of friends: one crying uncontrollably each night from the pain of urinary disease, another wasting away from consumption, pouring out blood. Dropsy and dysentery were ever present threats, and gangrene could mean a horrible death sentence, the pain dulled somewhat by endless bottles of red wine.[16] For life's minor miseries one was at the mercy of the bone-setters and tooth-pullers who rolled along to the local market or fair, and bleeders and quacks.

Plague loomed large in the popular consciousness. It came in irregular surges and although it was seen as a Divine punishment, a time for penitence and prayer, at the same time one was expected to take sensible precautions. God wanted us to protect ourselves 'both by his holy angels and by his healing gifts of medicine', as the sober advice given in Protestant Nuremberg had it: infected homes and clothes should be avoided, houses should be kept clean (not easy in winter, when spittle and urine collected on the floors and the walls), frequent bathing was commended, as was the chewing of garlic and the use of incense. Walking, exercise and drinking the waters were also commended, to drive out 'the great filth'. Heavy foods, and also giving way to anger, should both be avoided as dangerous to the health.[17]

[15] Ozment, *When Fathers Ruled*, p. 114.
[16] Ozment, *Magdalena and Balthasar*, p. 110.
[17] *Wie man sich in Zeit Regierender Pestilentz halten sol* (1562), quoted in Ozment, *Magdalena and Balthasar*, pp. 115ff.

Letter of Argula von Grumbach to her daughter, 1532

At times the concern for health could become somewhat obsessive. Magdalena Behaim was evangelical about bleeding. Balthasar worried continually about his stomach pains and his rheumatism and made regular pilgrimages to Carlsbad to take the waters. He hated it: 'in God's name. I am drinking, peeing, walking and sweating a lot' at the baths.[18]

Children, of course, were subject to coughs, headaches, lice, attacks of worms, all the adult ailments, but their health could deteriorate more quickly. Like Magdalena's son Balthasar they could be swept away by death almost overnight. It used to be argued that high mortality led to parental insensitivity to children's

[18]   Ozment, *Magdalena and Balthasar*, p. 134.

sufferings and deaths.[19] I have found no signs of this alleged indifference. Quite the opposite. In 1532, for example, Argula von Grumbach writes a moving letter to her daughter Appolonia, who has just recovered from fifty-one weeks' illness from the plague in distant Nuremberg:

> My dear daughter . . . I am so delighted you have taken a turn for the better . . . that the spots and pustules have disappeared, so follow the advice of your doctor and be grateful to God and to him; be godfearing, honest, patient and good . . .[20]

Magdalena Behaim was inconsolable after her little son Balthasar's death and referred to it again and again: 'there is nothing left in this life for me now except suffering, heartache, and tears. I must learn to block it from my mind as best I can . . . For me every day now becomes as three'[21] She finds some consolation in her little niece Madela: 'God preserve us, she is such a delightful thing . . . like a little monkey.' Parents may well have suffered as much for and with their children as they do today. It is surprising to learn that fathers were often expected to be present at a birth. They bought, or on occasion forgot to buy, toys for their children! Breughel's paintings, of course, remind us of the multitude of children's games.

There are also abundant signs of delight and pride in their children, mothers passing on their first cute phrases to fathers away from home. As a solo mother, Argula's letters sometimes had to strike a disciplinary tone, concerned that her boys work hard at their studies and keep out of trouble. Magdalena has the luxury of leaving that sort of thing to her husband, even quietly reproving male ambitions: 'Many fathers want more of their children than they often get.'[22] The warm tone of Argula's children in their letters

---

[19]   Philippe Aries, *Die Geschichte der Kindheit* (5th edition, Munich, 1982), p. 47.

[20]   Personenselekt Cat. 110 (Grombach).

[21]   Ozment, *Magdalena and Balthasar*, p. 101.

[22]   Ibid., p. 107.

to their mother is striking. They frequently show appreciation of efforts she has made for them and promise to requite it in due course, and work hard at their studies. Gottfried, for example, writes in 1538 to his 'most dear, heartily beloved lady mother', thanking her for her letter, the three cheeses, the New Testament in German, money and bedding:

> and I am studying and really working hard at my studies and you should have no doubt about it that if God gives me grace I will ensure that I grow up to be a good person, even if my brother doesn't turn out well.[23]

This is a reference to his brother Hans-Georg, of whom more later.

All four children were given a good education; her oldest son, George, had spent time at the Munich Court (presumably before the controversy about Seehofer), went to school in Nuremberg, finally studied in Wittenberg and was known to Luther and Melanchthon. It was a constant struggle, however, to pay for their fees, board and medical expenses, and provide school books, shoes, boots and clothing. Sometimes the letters contained desperate appeals for new clothes. A doublet had become ludicrously tight and small, for instance; the wardrobe was so small that hygiene at times seemed in considerable danger! There were surprising boyish requests for information about how to darn clothes. Argula made considerable efforts to visit them at distant Nuremberg or nearby Ingolstadt; she also found herself meeting the still more expensive cost of 'finishing school' at Protestant courts, where a veritable army of flunkeys had to be paid. Children left home at about seven. The cost of separation could be high as homesickness and difficulties with the strange diet and surroundings became too much for them, not to mention the expectations of the teacher. At times we sense the exhaustion of the single parent, expected to deal with everything, cope with complaints and bills, find energy for household affairs, manage the farm estates, deal with legal issues

---

[23]   Personenselekt Cat. 110 (Grombach).

and finance, oversee the children's upbringing and, in her spare time, advance the cause of the Reformation.

The teachers' understanding of education, as it emerges from these letters, was holistic, if narrow; pupils were boarded out with them or with their tutors, and their wives, who are frequently mentioned, would have played a major formative role. For schooling was not only about imparting knowledge – reading, writing, music, Latin, arithmetic – but also attended to the inculcation of life skills: if food gets lodged between the teeth at table, do not claw at it with the finger nails like a dog or cat; if possible, avoid urinating in public; stand up straight, and keep your hair neat; and, of course, learn honour, obedience, love.[24]

A letter by Argula's oldest son, George, writing from school in Nuremberg in 1525 at the height of the Peasants' War, testifies to the success of such education. It reported with impressive maturity on the turmoil in the city and the dismissal for Anabaptism of George's teacher, Hans Denck, whom he obviously liked; although he wrote to both parents, his language was evangelical in flavour, and reflected his mother's concerns.[25]

But four years later his teacher Ketzmann wrote two furious letters to his parents. As soon as his mother had left Nuremberg, George had beetled off to the pub with his uncle Bernhardin. Worse still, after a home visit to his father he had returned without any readiness for work or discipline.

> If he is to continue as my pupil he will have to eat humble pie like everyone else, so that the evil he is so full of can be punished. If he doesn't learn this in his youth he will be a slave to evil in his maturity and reveal his lack of self-knowledge.

This can sound more draconian than it was in reality. Her children's teachers, such as Johann Ketzmann, were aware of the need to motivate and gain the cooperation of the home, and that 'swingeing punishment doesn't achieve much': '*Munter straff richt*

---

[24]   Ozment, *When Fathers Ruled*, p. 138.
[25]   Personenselekt Cat. 110 (Grombach).

bey den sinnen nit vill auss.' Gottfried, his teacher Jakob reports, is not doing at all badly; if necessary he will not spare the rod, but the boy seems quite willing and so he won't push him too hard; he has reduced his dairy cheese intake on the doctor's advice as he had been troubled by headaches.[26]

Ozment argues that the rigour of the teachers rested on the need to train their pupils for social duty and the salvation of their soul.[27] In Argula von Grumbach's case it was part of a grim struggle in which mother, teacher, and pastor joined forces against the crude, hard-drinking, devil-may-care ethos of the lesser nobility. There was a continual struggle against the conventional mores of the nobility: drinking, hunting, brawling, whoring. It may be easy to sneer at this as puritanical, but such traditional conduct reduced many women's and children's lives to misery. There are hints both in the published and private writings of Argula von Grumbach that domestic violence was never far away from any woman's life, and one of her reforming concerns had been to raise standards of literacy and reflectiveness among the nobility.

Adam von Grumbach's son 'is a real peasant, a typical Grumbach', writes her son George, who had been dragged along willy-nilly to the local Kirmes or parish carnival, always an excuse for revelry of the most unsophisticated kind. One wonders, given a comment such as this, what he thought of his own father! Another more notorious relative was Wilhelm von Grumbach, who provided absolutely no assistance to Argula, and indeed personified the anachronistic, swashbuckling world of the lesser nobility. He engaged in dynastic feuds and anti-clerical intrigues for his own financial ends, and ended, predictably perhaps, by being executed for treason, with awesome cruelty even by our twentieth-century standards.[28]

Thus Argula's costly investment in education was part of her Lutheranism, but also part of the desperate struggle to enable her

---

[26]   Ibid.
[27]   *When Fathers Ruled*, p. 171.
[28]   Volker Press, 'Wilhelm von Grumbach', esp. pp. 413f.

children to climb up out of the mire by means of tough discipline, and to see a wider world. The constant danger of her own children sliding down into this world was highlighted by her promising son George being dreadfully wounded in Leipzig in 1533, presumably in a fight; he never really recovered. The last letter relating to him is poignant indeed: a request from a Leipzig inn-keeper to pay the debts of her dead son, incurred as he lay sick.[29] Surprisingly, given the emperor's anti-Lutheran stance, the old patriotic values seemed to have remained unquestioned in her household. Her second son, Hans-Georg, rushed off enthusiastically to enrol in the emperor's war against the French in 1531.

Gottfried, who proved to be the only child to outlive his mother, was the most conscientious. His letters were full of phrases invoking the help and the grace of God, which no doubt mirrored in a childlike way his mother's piety. He was full of good will and honourable intentions. He wrote rather pathetic letters to his older brother Hans-Georg complaining at his failure to keep in touch, and begging him to stop telling lies and to avoid creating scandal; he should start behaving, be *frum und zuchtig*.[30] One mysterious incident involving Hans-Georg appears to have been of a criminal nature, because his mother insisted on total secrecy:

> Grace and peace to you, my dear son. I was terribly shocked to hear about what happened at Burggrumbach from your letter, and before that from [other] people. I have been agonised by it, and I go on lamenting in my prayers to God that the children I have borne and nourished at my breast and raised with such great worry, cost and anxiety have proved so disobedient. God grant that you may repent and improve in the future, Amen. Since, however, you are now writing and asking me to forgive you, and are promising obedience in the future, I will do so just once more, providing you adhere to my instructions and disciplines and find a way to settle the matter.

29 Personenselekt Cat. 110 (Grombach).
30 Ibid.

So see to it that you come home at once, though you are not to come until you have taken the sacrament at Nuremberg. Go to Dr Osiander, and tell him penitently what happened, and what you are asking of him; he will certainly know what advice to give you to put your conscience to rest. So don't try to keep anything back from him; he already knows about the affair. And on your life see that you tell no one anything about it, trust no one and keep the matter absolutely secret. And when you have received the sacrament, ask Osiander to certify this, otherwise I won't believe you. Get an account from the landlord also of your food bill in Nuremberg and of any previous debts to him, and have him itemise everything exactly, and bring it with you. Tell Gottfried that he should study hard, and stick to his lessons and not run around in the town or in the pubs, that he should pay good attention to the preaching and remain truly upright and obedient [frum]. God be gracious to you, then. Lenting, Wednesday after Easter, 1538.[31]

The whole incident was typical of her iron will and the uphill struggle to mediate cultural and religious goals. Her whole life is something of an eye-opener about the realities of personal life in the early days of the Reformation. It leaves no room for confessional triumphalism, especially from the perspective of women.

Yet Argula's achievements were not negligible. She fought her way back from despair. She overcame personal tragedy and the collapse of many of her social and ecclesiastical dreams. There was an impressive concentration on the achievable. She won respect for herself as a woman, a lay exegete of Scripture, a mother, a neighbour. She created space for family, friends and clients to explore a better future. She left behind her little Lutheran enclaves and the memory of a life of quite exceptional courage, both of which were to survive the centuries, and she explored in an imaginative way new contours of personal life.

[31]   Ibid.

CHAPTER SIX

THE SPIRITUALITY
OF THE REFORMATION

'Tradition', Jaroslav Pelikan has finely said, 'is the living faith of the dead; traditionalism, the dead faith of the living.'[1] Protestantism, or neo-Protestantism as we call the modification of Reformation heritage by the Enlightenment and the nineteenth-century revolutions, is manifestly in deepest crisis. Yet a premature concern to recover its Reformation heritage seems invariably to lead to a romantic distortion, while a self-limiting ordinance to uncover and analyse the Reformation keeps us at an ironic distance from its most urgent concerns.

We began this book with Edwin Muir's question about the odour of ancient bibles, about imagination as the Achilles heel of Protestantism. I have suggested that it is possible to revisit the Reformation, seeing it less as a doctrinal shift or structural upheaval, though it was both of these, than as an event in the imagination, a shift in the basic paradigms through which people perceived their world. My hope is that in this way we may get closer to it and it may in turn touch us at a deeper level. If this is true, it should be indicated above all in its spirituality.

Spirituality is a much-used, perhaps over-used, word. Here it indicates the areas of worship, personal piety and life-style. Clearly we can only make a few tentative probes into the mass of material open to us: liturgies, hymns, prayers, sermons and letters. I will begin by indicating in broad brush strokes some of the key issues,

---

[1] Jaroslav Pelikan, *The Vindication of Tradition* (New Haven and London: Yale University Press, 1984).

and then seek to illustrate, in what will necessarily be an impressionistic way, the approach of Luther and the radicals, and the emergent patterns of family piety.

Let us acknowledge first of all that the heritage the Reformation left behind was an ambiguous one: side by side with a dramatic rediscovery of Scripture and a renewal of virtually all aspects of church life, it created a sundered Church, bleak habits of mutual distrust and contempt and, although much that is attributed to the Reformation truly belongs to the following confessional and Puritan era, what has been described as a stripping of the altars culturally, liturgically and cultically, a Lenten exegesis of the Gospel. The anticlerical and apocalyptic currents that launched the Reformation were to linger on in anachronistic, secularised form to haunt the crabbed minds of populist politicians throughout the Western world for centuries to come. The freight train of the Reformation also bore along with it, in many cases, antisemitic ecstasies which ensure that to this day Jewish scholarship has found it almost impossible to enter its imaginative world.

As we near the end of the millennium, it may be timely for us to revisit the era of the Renaissance and Reformation, the hinge for what we still call modernity, the last five hundred years of our European history, though we should have no illusions that the process will be undialectical or the answers simple. To mention only two points. Ours is an eminently non-Utopian time to be alive. Our generation is struggling with the apparent disintegration of virtually every social ideal our parents sought to foster, and with the relentless commodification of education itself. Access to the sixteenth-century world is particularly difficult under such circumstances. Secondly, our cultural perspective determines what we perceive. The clash between American and European historians is always an illuminating one. To give another example, the Pacific perspective of my Maori, Samoan, Cook Island and Niuean students in New Zealand led them to address very different questions to the various reformations of the sixteenth century from those to which I had been accustomed. They were, for example, closer to its corporate spirituality than our individualist European traditions.

Reformation spirituality, then. Was it, as is so often suggested, a shift from a visual and celebratory culture to a verbal and pedagogic one, from a more feminine to a more patriarchal mode, from a communal religiosity to a decidedly individualistic one? Was the Reformation a medically-indicated intervention in a dramatically sick body, as Lazarus Spengler suggested, or the destabilisation of an intact body? Part of the answer to such questions will be determined by whether we are structuralists like the Annales school, viewing history as determined by the ongoing continuities of demography and geography and macro-economic trends; or whether, like the post-modernists, we prefer to eschew all grand narratives and focus on pluralisms, variations and regional nuances; or whether, a third option, we leave more room for human intervention, even on the grand scale, and presuppose the pre-eminence of the catastrophic and the redemptive.[2] This latter, more crisis-ridden, view is much favoured by Marxists and is, I believe, also closest to the self-understanding of the Reformers. A working historian like myself will want to combine some awareness of long term trends with a respect for shorter term contingencies and a recognition of multiplicities and provincial nuances, but we may have to take note that the oppressed of the world, who in my reading of history have always been the over-whelming majority, have consistently favoured the catastrophe/redemption model. Where spirituality operated as a mask for the economic and cultural violation of the credulous by the clergy, it was perceived as quite peculiarly oppressive.

Hence it need not surprise us that it was Luther's devotional literature, rather than his reform programmes or doctrinal tracts,

---

[2]   The papers of the 1996 symposium of the Verein für Reformations-geschichte, gathered together in *Die frühe Reformation in Deutschland als Umbruch* offer the best recent discussion of these issues; cf. the helpful warnings against 'loading' the Reformation with the responsibility for modernity, p. 488.

which won for him the hearts of the German people, as Mark Edwards, among others, has recently demonstrated.[3] Why? In what sense did it offer them liberation and deliverance?

Simplicity is often at the heart of genius. Luther reached straight to the heart of things, disregarding all peripheral issues and fussy details. In his *Ein seer gut und nutzlichs Bettbuchleyn*, a very popular and influential book of prayers for lay people (which he pronounced good and useful in comparison to the dead wood previously trundled out),[4] his aim was to provide an alternative to a calculating piety which weighed sins against merits and sought to insure against failure by multiplying devotional exercises and good works. This was to seduce the simple. He laid bare, therefore, the traditional sinews of piety: the Ten Commandments, the Creed and the Lord's Prayer, removing legendary accretions and all *Überfluss*, or superfluity of words. What God really wanted from us was our sighs and tears.

An image, Ezra Pound has said, 'presents an intellectual and emotional complex in an instant of time'. It was the images of the heart which had to be replaced, Luther insisted, not outward images. He reworked the Ten Commandments, for example, with an inventive generosity which reminded this reader of Jesus' reinterpretation of the Torah. We are not here on this earth to honour ourselves or likenesses of ourselves but only what is worthy of honour. God is redefined in terms of the one to whom alone honour is due. The 'You shall nots' of the Commandments are swallowed up by their positive inversions: slander, for example, is trumped by a disposition to think the best of others, to blanket their faults with forgetfulness. The Psalms, which Luther loved so much as peerless barometers of the human heart, leapt out of his translations in sparkling, associative, direct, vernacular language, as urgent in their rhythms as rap, his reverent irreverence

---

[3]   'Thanks to these largely pastoral and devotional works, Luther became Germany's first best-selling vernacular author'; *Printing, Propaganda and Martin Luther*, p. 164.

[4]   W 10/II, pp. 375–482.

rediscovering them as the wild poetry and lyrical yearning which they are.

Piety shifted gear, then, from prudent or anxious negotiation with a calculating Deity to an overdrive of thanksgiving, from a awe-struck adoration of the Mass to pursuing its fruits in daily life. How does it help you that God is God, Luther asks, if God is not God for you? Attending Mass is not the point; true Christians are those who pull Christ's life and name into their lives. Simple, graphic images!

Don't focus on externals such as the crown of thorns, he urged, with Lent in mind; it is your inner self which tortures Christ; engrave that deeply in your inmost being. We need self-knowledge; we need to let the suffering of Christ work in us sacramentally.

On Easter Day, however, we can shake out our sins on Christ, and leave them there, push right through the pain of Christ to his friendly heart and, beyond it, to the divine heart, the kindly Father, boldly believing that by Christ's resurrection our sins are buried and our old humanity immersed, drowned in the flood of grace which is Baptism.

Engrave it deeply into your very being! Shake it all out! Boldly believe! The religious imagination is being refocused here. Biblical metaphors are being nudged, teased, eased into new shape and priorities upended. The scattered kaleidoscopic fragments of the old religious imagination re-emerge in patterns of unpredicted and unpredictable beauty. Interiority was a mark of Luther's spirituality, as of so many of the late medieval reformers and mystics. There is continuity here as well as a new symbolic universe, a fresh choreography for a daily rule of life.

Was this the advent of a verbal rather than a visual spirituality? The priority given to Scripture and sermon might seem to make this question redundant, but caution is in place. What is word, what is image? Perhaps the Reformers are best understood as Deuteronomists, post-exilic purgers of the sanctuary.[5] In an

---

[5]   Thomas Müntzer, for example, explicitly refers to Josiah's reforms: CW, 100.

intriguing new book, *The Image and the Book*,[6] Karel van der Toorn questions the assumption that faith in Jahweh, Israel's God, was always free of images, graven or otherwise. He also suggests that the Deuteronomic reform made Torah itself into something of an image, an icon which was elevated in worship, borne into battle, worn around the body, fastened to the doorpost. If, as van der Toorn argues, the chasm between image and book can be exaggerated; if images have to be 'read', and are themselves a sort of 'text'; if canonical books, on the other hand, are treated with such reverence that they 'defile the hands' and become themselves a sort of icon; then Reformation spirituality also may have been the replacement of one symbolic world by another, not an assault on symbolism as such. Was the Reformation attack on the veneration of Mary and the saints similar to the Deuteronomic assault on Asherah? As Paul Ricoeur points out, every symbol is iconoclastic against a previous one. Were the Reformers so different from the Jerusalem priests who, following the Deuteronomic reform, monopolised the interpretation of Torah? Luther's radical opponents, who liked to attack him as the New Pope, certainly seem to have seen him in this way.

What constituted this new symbolic world? Ultimately the power of the religious imagination of the Reformation, its light, truth, fertility, freshness and healing energy, sprang from what the Reformers called the living Word of God: the Law and the prophets, the evangelists and apostles, their hymns, poetry, psalms, stories, metaphors, parables, paradoxes. But of course this Bible was read contextually. Those who read it in a workshop saw different things there from the reforming sympathiser in a monastery. Chrisman has pointed out how differently Scripture was used. For the culturally deprived it could be virtually their only book. 82% of artisans used scriptural references in their pamphlets, 45% of patricians, and only 24% of the nobility.[7]

---

[6]   K. van der Toorn (ed.), *The Image and the Book. Iconic Cults, Aniconism and the Rise of Book Religion in Israel and the Ancient Near East* (Leuven: Peeters, 1997), esp. pp. 229, 254.

[7]   Chrisman, *Conflicting Visions*, p. 10.

The patriarchal metaphor in the Bible was one of the key categories which resonated with Luther's hearers. The patriarchal prince, pastor, master-craftsman and father took his cue from Luther's kindly God–Father. God as patriarch was a considerable advance on God as avenger. In an age where patriarchal is a 'hiss-word', we do well to remember that. But the pathetic little refugee groups heading for Moravia in the sixteenth century clutched in their hands the Zurich Bible, and clutched to their hearts the communal dream, for 'this was their story, this was their song', one of sisterhood and brotherhood not of patriarchy. Hence we have to be cautious that we do not read the evidence with a tunnel vision that sees only the patriarchical elements in the Reformation but misses the prophetic, evangelical, apostolic models in sermons and pamphlets and the influence of the Wisdom writings. We are in danger of 'selecting out' here, failing to read against the grain of our ingrained good consciences. After all, the prophetic passion of an Argula von Grumbach sprang straight from her reading of Isaiah or Joel; the first vernacular German Mass by Thomas Müntzer came from his revelling in the earliest, apostolic Church; the evangelical warmth of Martin Bucer was stoked by his love of the Gospels. The biblical models danced out of the pages for them.

This did not mean, of course, that they read the Bible biblicistically. Luther, Zwingli, Calvin were all humanists. The unravelling of the images of Scripture implied a love of the languages, a sensitivity to syntax, a historical empathy which flowed from humanism – the best scholarship of the day. Parents and kinsfolk of limited or threadbare resources stretched their hearts as well as their pockets to enable their children to study, to have access to the original texts. The biblical humanists propounded an intelligible and intelligent piety. They harboured suspicion less of symbols as such than of their unreflective use, and of that glandular excess in worship which scholars such as Bullinger saw as the root of all superstition. Good people, he felt, tended to let their enthusiasms run away with them, unchecked by biblical norms, and the result was catastrophic. Piety had to be theologically controlled. G. H. Williams pointed out long ago

that the aim of Protestant academies from Strasbourg to Geneva
to Harvard was to revive the prophetic colleges of ancient Israel,
in the hope that a disciplined imagination would recreate something of the pure contours of paradise. The world of John Milton
is not far from us here.[8]

With the Bible and humanism went a reaffirmation of the
vernacular, as so often in the Renaissance. To read the prophets
in Luther's or Zwingli's German was a revelation to people,
not only because, as is rightly stressed, they really understood
them but because the nuances of Scripture were caught in the
intimate and familiar rhythms of market-place and kitchen. It
must have been very like what I feel when reading Lorimer's
New Testament in Scots. There is a swingeing relish in raw
rhetoric, in the language which flows from the guts, an elemental
surge of pain and yearning and *ecstasis* in worship, *im schwanck*
Müntzer calls it, which is not so far removed from the language
of Shakespeare, not to mention Rabelais, and is certainly related
to them. The dams of polite Latinate convention had been burst
for ever.

Religious language, at its best, is always primal, and in the
best sense of the word, vulgar, common to us all. Birth and death
are vulgar, pain is vulgar, evil is vulgar, sex is vulgar, violence is
vulgar. At the beginning of this century Karl Holl, so instrumental
in the Luther renaissance, noted the importance of worldly
holiness for Luther's religion of conscience, a spirituality grounded
in daily life and relationships. The humblest tasks in this world,
if seen as service of your neighbour, as fulfilling your God-
given vocation, are more pleasing to God that the otherworldli-
ness of the monastic ideal.[9] Dietrich Bonhoeffer also drew on
that source. It proved the deadly foe of all sentimentality, and was

---

[8]   G. H. Williams, *Wilderness and Paradise in Christian Thought; the biblical
experience of the desert in the history of Christianity and the paradise theme in the
theological idea of the university* (New York: Harper, 1962).

[9]   Karl Holl, *Gesammelte Aufsätze zue Kirchengeschichte* 1 (7th edition;
Tübingen: J. C. B. Mohr, 1948), esp. pp. 102, 258–60.

the soul-sister of that precision and tenderness which Kurt Marti calls love.[10]

The Reformers not only revered their biblical heritage, but recovered its energies, its acids, its spices, its 'red wine and cheese', the sting and zing of the Magnificat. We should therefore be chary of assuming that a more verbal spirituality, which Protestantism undoubtedly was, was necessarily more bookish or intellectual. It commuted between the lofty discourse of the classics and the rude simplicities of the vernacular. The living Word which Luther was talking about, emerged from a filthy stable and ended on a foul cross. Theology was worked out in the study, certainly, but above all in living, dying, being damned.[11] *Theologia crucis*.

As indulgences, relics, pilgrimages and confraternities disappeared, new ways had to be found for lay people to bond with one another, although of course in rural areas particularly, the old ways died hard, and a slow process of compromise and acculturation took place. Again, remarkably little attention has been given to the way in which this was done. In the early days of the Reformation there are references to gatherings in artisans' workshops, Thomas Müntzer's 'upper room'; women's groups met in the *Spinnstuben* and one another's homes, to discuss the faith, or to hear readings from the latest pamphlet. We may have underestimated the extent to which the values of the community were defended and developed by subtle and not so subtle social pressures exercised by parishioners themselves. Social conformity was by no means carried out only from above.

The nobleman Ekhardt zum Drübel speaks for many lay people: 'I can and may, I and every Christian, write, sing, talk, advise, speak, teach, instruct in a Christian way.'[12] People helped

---

[10] Kurt Marti, *Zart und genau. Reflexionen Geschichten Gedichte Predigten* (ed. Siegfried Bräuer and Hansjürgen Schulz; Berlin: Evangelische Verlagsanstalt, 1985).

[11] 'Vivendo, immo moriendo et damnando fit theologus, non intelligendo, legendo aut speculando.' WA 5, 153/28.

[12] '*Ein vetterliche gedruge gute zucht, lere und bericht*', fols. Diiv–Diiiv, quoted in Chrisman, *Conflicting Visions*, p. 102.

one another out at times of bereavement with visits and little presents of cheese or wine. Early Anabaptism's popularity may have to be seen in this context of the need for mutual support and encouragement. Amongst radical and reformed groups, the covenant of the elect, to which people on occasion actually signed their names, was of course a highly significant phenomenon, a committing of themselves in writing to one another and to the cause. Some lay people would exercise a role as magistrates, lawyers, *Kirchenpfleger* or elders. Martin Bucer was one of the few clerical leaders with an awareness of the need to develop such fellowship, though there was a general awareness of the need to gather the more conscientious members as an *ecclesiola in ecclesia*.

As we turn to the radical variants of Protestantism, using the example of Thomas Müntzer, the vernacular dimension to piety became still more dominant. In no way, however, did this exclude gentleness:

> O Lord, bestow on us the grace of the Holy Spirit, so that the dew of your goodness may sprinkle the very depths of our heart and make it bring forth good fruit through Jesus [Christ our Lord].

Or take this verse from his lovely communion hymn:

> Here was ground the grain of wheat
> Which the cost of sin did meet.
> Here was broken life's true bread,
> As the prophets had foresaid.
> Bread for living
> Christ's the giving
> Here, upon a sore Cross stretching.[13]

Müntzer's liturgy shuns the magical incantations of Latin, purges away all the mumbo jumbo, as he puts it. He seeks a linguistic immediacy which will enable the Light of the world to shine forth

---

[13]   CW, pp. 399f.

through hymns and godly songs.[14] It is crammed with temporal, spatial and inter-personal images.

Müntzer regarded public worship, in its preaching, singing and sacraments, as a training ground for the elect, for their edification and growth, for the formation of the new humanity. His concept of the 'lazy elect', who had to be pricked and prodded into an awareness of their awesome calling, warns us against equating pre-destinarian views with fatalism, or even with a denial of free will.

There was also a powerful communal dimension. The elements of the Eucharist are consecrated by the priest but blessed, corporately, by the whole gathered congregation. Christ was not a 'painted puppet' to be conjured up by a priestly incantation. Likewise the whole community exercised the power of the keys, the ministry of deliverance. This assault on clerical privilege led to the accusation by opponents 'that we teach even yokels from the fields to celebrate Mass'.[15]

On one level we can see this as a form of lay empowerment. But for Müntzer, and many other radical preachers, the point was really quite different. Genuine discipleship was seen as a calling for all without exception. The real stumbling block to under-standing the Gospel was not our coarseness, our lack of academic training, but our sophistication, what today we would call, perhaps, our ironic detachment, our bookishness. Similarly, Karlstadt gave up his academic gown for peasant garb. For him the whole congregation was to be alert and active, not passive, members of Christ, ready to exercise righteousness.[16] Worship was participatory training for life. Radical liturgies therefore flowed into radical action. *The Swiss Order* (1527) saw breaking the bread together as a commitment to having all things in common in the whole of life and a readiness to be torn apart in martyrdom, 'that

[14] CW, p. 166.
[15] CW, p. 174.
[16] *'glidmaß zu der gerechtigkeit bereit'*; *Ob man gemach faren/ und des ergernissen die schwachen verschonen soll/ in sachen so gottis willen angehen* (Basel, 1524), Bii.

we might also be willing to give our body and life for Christ's sake, which means for the sake of all the brothers'.[17] Christ was present in the living bodies of the people of God, not in the elements of bread and wine. Worship dramatised this liminality and communality of the whole of life.

Locher, for example, asked how the oppression of the poor could continue in society when all Christians ate the Lord's Supper together. 'Don't we eat the one bread? Don't we drink with one cup the cross of Christ?'[18] The woods, the rivers, the fields, *omnia sunt communa*, all are to be held in common, because they are all sacred. In the *ordo rerum*, the divine order of things, we who are possessed of God possess all these as not possessing them. Maori, aboriginal people instinctively know what is being talked about here. We belong to the land, and not vice versa.

Part of what was lost by the suppression of what, following Blickle, we have called the communal reformation, was this egalitarianism in worship and the critique of a bookish faith; also lost was something of this sense of the continuum between worship and life, the sacred and the secular. For women, what was lost was a recognition that Baptism swept aside all the gender constructs of the threatened male mind. It is interesting to remember who kept the memory of Reformation women leaders alive – not the liberals, the modernists, or the super-orthodox, but the often derided Pietists![19]

Personal Piety

We are still very far from having an overall perspective on the personal piety of this period, partly because social historians do not read church historians and vice versa, partly because the evidence is fragmentary and allusive. My impressions are that it is

---

[17]   Quoted in Packull, *Hutterite Beginnings*, p. 311.

[18]   Johannes Locher, *Second Letter to Karsthans*, p. 100 (my translation).

[19]   Cf. Georg Rieger, *Das Leben Argulae von Grumbach gebohrner von Stauffen als einer Jüngerin Jesu, Zeugin der Warheit und Freundin Lutheri . . .* (Stuttgart: Metzler & Erhard, 1737).

often remarkably natural and unforced, avoiding cloying sentimentalism, and the need to lace every communication with pious sub-texts.[20] On the other hand, the decline into legalism can be quite rapid. We are told that Bucer's household in Cambridge, for example, groaned at his rigorous disciplines. Justification by faith was easier as a doctrine, it seems, than applied to daily life. It has been noted that ethical rigorism often accompanied a high doctrine of grace.[21]

Scripture, of course, was central to personal piety. The paterfamilias, off on his business travels, is asked, 'Please send us the Old Testament with the Psalms and the Prophets, for we often need it.'[22] Above all, the Psalms became the centre-piece of lay worship. Writing to his sister Hilgart in 1524, an unknown pastor offers her a whole pattern for personal devotion based on the Psalms. The woodcut on the printed version features David as the model of the contrite sinner. The pastor commends seven penitential psalms if her conscience is heavy laden, hastening to add that she doesn't need to repeat them all in one day! The Psalms are also a source for thanksgiving, comfort and strength against one's enemies. The images of deliverance are particularly vivid. The Word of God is a powerful fire, a hammer and sword which destroys death, the devil, and all our enemies. The warm emotional tone, the love, praise, fear and honour for God are striking. 'Feed my spirit with the power of your living Word.'[23] In the light of the prevalence of such prayers, the sweeping judgements often made in recent times (by, for example, Bossy and McLaughlin) about Protestant piety replacing an immanentist piety with a lofty, male, transcendental one seem questionable.

[20]   Kolman Grasser, one of Argula's correspondents, is an exception; Personenselekt Cat. 110 (Grombach).
[21]   H. R. Schmidt talks of a *'sanative Rechtfertigungsvorstellung'*: 'Die Ethik der Laien in der Reformation', *Die frühe Reformation in Deutschland als Umbruch*, pp. 333–70.
[22]   Ozment, *Magdalena and Balthasar*, p. 89.
[23]   Chrisman, *Conflicting Visions*, pp. 99f.; Chrisman believes it is a woman author, but clearly the writer is a man, probably a pastor.

Recent research on the motif of God's accommodation to us in the thought of Calvin also suggests that such judgements are in need of qualification.

Lutheran piety was domestic as well as scriptural. It centred around the home, although for some decades this tended to be restricted to the professional and upper classes. People would gather around to sing hymns and read books and prayers: *Gesang, Gebet, Lektüre.* Regular attendance at preaching, the Lord's Supper and confession (for confession continued in many Lutheran areas) was frequently supplemented by what Patrice Veit characterises as quite strongly ritualised family prayers, as well as people's private devotions. They would take place each day, but especially on Saturday evening and before church on Sunday morning.[24]

The father of the household was expected to make his home a church, echoing the intentions of Luther, Karlstadt and other Reformers. Karlstadt, for example, recommended that 'all housefathers should apply themselves diligently to learn God's word, so that they may instruct their children'.[25] He was to be the messenger (*Bote*) of God, the *Hausprediger* or house-preacher, leading the systematic bible reading, the prayers, the singing of chorales. The prayer book or hymn book became a well-thumbed, sentimental possession, which was sometimes taken to the grave.

This may indeed appear to be a very bookish piety, but one should remember that it was relatively common for chapters of Scripture and many of the Psalms to be learnt off by heart. Prayers and readings would be interrupted by groans and sighs. Luther himself was often observed in tears as he read his Psalms or said

---

[24]   Patrice Veit, 'Private Frömmigkeit, Lekture und Gesang im protestantischen Deutschland der frühen Neuzeit: das Modell der Leichenpredigten', in *Frühe Neuzeit – Frühe Moderne? Forschungen zue Vielschichtigkeit von Übergangsprozessen* (ed. Rudolf Vierhaus; Veröff. d. Max-Planck-Instituts für Geschichte, 104; Göttingen: Vandenhoeck & Ruprecht, 1992), pp. 271–95.

[25]   *Predig oder homilien uber den propheten, Malachiam gnant,* Aiiii r., quoted in Preus, *Carlstadt's Ordinaciones . . . ,* p. 50.

his prayers.[26] There was a warm emotional tone about Lutheran devotions. Popular proverbs, typically wielded by the mother of the house, also helped to anchor piety in reality. *Wie der Grund, so das Geben*. 'Know the soil, know what springs from it', as Argula von Grumbach put it in her letter to Adam von Thering.[27] This extended family, which included the servants as well as relatives, reminds us that such piety was not individualistic

The mother, the *Hauspredigerin*, had primary responsibility for the children, especially the girls. Boys left home for school or tutoring or a relative's home very early, at 6 or 7 years old, but girls would generally remain with their mother until they were married. Spinning and weaving would sometimes be accompanied by hymns or bible-reading, an antidote to the livelier *Spinnstuben*, spinning circles notorious for their gossip and racy songs, not to mention other worrying goings-on!

There are signs that women's religiosity tended to be more developed than that of the men. Argula von Grumbach hinted that the Bavarian nobility, in particularly, could have taken a few lessons from their more reflective and literate womenfolk.[28] Men preferred, it seems, the sermon collections and the more credal hymns; women the books of edification and the more personal hymns.

By the end of the century books of edification comprised about 25% of the total German book production: bibles, catechisms, hymn books, collections of prayers and sermons. From about 1580 the custom developed of having necrologies printed, idealised depictions of the departed which themselves then became part of

---

[26]   Cf. Melanchthon's comments at Luther's funeral: 'I often came upon him saying his prayers for the whole church while hot tears ran down his face. For he took specific time for himself each day to repeat some Psalms, mingling with them his prayers to God with sighs and tears.' *Vom Christlichen abschied* . . . , p. 89 (my translation).

[27]   'wie der grundt also dass geben'; *Argula von Grumbach*, p. 146. I am indebted to Alejandro Zorzin for this translation, which corrects my previous one.

[28]   AvG, pp. 79f., 146–8.

the process of Christianisation. They became immensely popular, being a substitute for the traditional masses for the dead.

People also began gathering their own personal notebooks or 'treasuries' of favourite texts, prayers and hymns. These patterns of domestic piety then spread down to the rest of society through Pietism. There is, however, considerable evidence throughout the sixteenth century of stubborn resistance, especially in rural areas, to catechising and similar expectations of home-based piety, as indeed to church-going itself, though the rich and growing selection of Lutheran hymns proved particularly popular.[29] Long after Müntzer's death his hymns were sung, and Anabaptist groups such as the Philipites were famous for their hymns.

In terms of individual piety, Müntzer offered one of the most interesting experiments in propagating a popular mysticism, a profound personal piety for every believer. Many of his letters are what today we would call spiritual counselling for lay people. Faith is here and now. God is near at hand. John the Baptist does not roam the Judaean desert but the desert of our souls. Christ has to be reborn not in Nazareth but in the abyss, the deepest ground of our being – a painful and personal process which cannot be short-circuited. 'Anyone who rejects the bitter Christ will gorge himself to death on honey.'[30] In other words, every Christian is called to experience the heights and depths of doubt and despair as well as knowledge and faith. Pastors and theologians cannot fob off lay people with mere formulae, however biblically correct, a second-hand, second-best, mediated, counterfeit faith. Christ does not call us to be parrots.

Except to designate the days of the year, saints were scarcely mentioned any more. Among lay people you seldom come across any mention of Mary. 'Do *not* greet the saints or ask them for enlightenment', as Otto Brunfels' handbook for bringing up

---

[29]   Cf. C. Scott Dixon, *The Reformation and Rural Society. The Parishes of Brandenburg-Ansbach-Kulmbach 1528–1603* (Cambridge Studies in Early Modern History; Cambridge, 1996).

[30]   CW, p. 220.

children emphatically insists.[31] There seems much less mention, too, of angels, who had played such a key role in personal piety before. Sometimes the elect, as God's messengers, are addressed as angels and, of course, as God's saints.

To meet the precariousness and unpredictability of life, people resorted to prayer, but mobilised what resources and energies they had at their command as well, doing their own sensible best. As Ozment succinctly puts it, 'The imagination and the energy for their undertakings were self-consciously their own, but God invariably got the credit for the outcome in recognition of his sovereignty over life.'[32] Everything was attributed to God's will, which they might not always be able to fathom, of course, but which was seen to be working for truth and justice in the end.

This is a very common-sense point of view which integrates spirituality with daily life, with the activities and precautions of the thoughtful citizen or country-dweller. In view of the current vogue for the more exotic features of popular religion, it is interesting that I have yet to find in such private letters (which, of course, tend to come from the upper classes) any mention of magical or cabbalistic practices, of wise women or witchcraft, white or black. The strong belief in God's overarching providence may have left little room for Satan. Certainly, by the beginning of the seventeenth century Nuremberg's preachers would be pooh-poohing the powers of witches as pure blindness and delusion.

Changing images

How did the way in which God was viewed change?

God the Father remained the God of judgement, the God of power and justice whose cause would win out in the end, who

---

[31] *Von der Zucht der Kinder* (Strasburg, 1525); on the other hand respect and reverence for the saints as models of discipleship was fostered by Protestant collections on the lives of the saints.

[32] Ozment, *Magdalena and Balthasar*, p. 154.

must be properly honoured and obeyed, socially and individually, or the consequences would be painfully felt. But he was also the kindly patriarch.

Christ, as we have seen, had come closer to humanity. He was no longer the remote and terrible Judge. Children were to think of Christ as 'their best, their most faithful, their friendliest friend'.[33] Peasants were depicted as greeting their dear lord Jesus Christ, who proclaimed good news not to bishops but to peasants and simple folk. He was their Captain (*haubtman*) in the battle to create a just society.[34] Argula von Grumbach emphasised the teachings of Jesus, and that his way is not coercive but humble and supportive. In Christ we see God's protective care for us, like a hen caring for its chicks. We see him weeping over Jerusalem.[35] Balthasar Paumgartner writes a Christmas letter wishing his bride to be 'a Happy New Year, through Jesus Christ, the newborn child, our only Saviour, redeemer and Sanctifier'.[36]

It may be that the insistence on *Christus solus*, our only saviour, not only states the theological principle that he alone is our mediator and that there is no need for the intercession of Mary and the saints, but also serves to inculcate self-reliance. After this great spring cleaning of superfluous hierarchies of helpers, we are more or less on our own and have to 'get on with it', taking sensible precautions about our health or welfare. Heide Wunder has suggested that Luther's use of *fromm* as a German rendering for the Latin *iustus*, or righteous, brought into spirituality the world of associations from ordinary civic life which clustered around *fromm*, such as upright, reliable, honourable. The dichotomy between the inner or ascetic world of the spirit and the outer, material world of work and neighbourliness

---

[33]   Eberlin von Günzburg, *Ein schöner Speigel des christlichen Lebens*, quoted in Ozment, *When Fathers Ruled*, p. 172.

[34]   Locher, *Second Letter to Karsthans*, pp. 965/17.

[35]   Cf. my article 'A Reformation for women? Sin, grace and gender in Argula von Grumbach', *Scottish Journal of Theology* 49/1 (1996), pp. 39–55.

[36]   Ozment, *Magdalena and Balthasar*, p. 28.

disappears.[37] A disenchanted world, free of a prodigious clutter of saints and demons, left more room for pragmatic, secular decisions.

There are, of course, countless references to the Holy Spirit ('Ach, pour your holy spirit into my dark, sinful heart'), but on the whole those to the living Word of God, 'truly a great fire', or as light, power, truth, are more vigorous and innovative.

How different was people's image of the Church? It was less clerical, less institutional. The people of God were God's true temples. The Christian Church, the artisan Bastian Goltschmidt told his Dominican opponent, is not in stones or a cloister; it is gathered by God's Word.[38] Hergot's name for the leaders of the community, *gotteshaws ernerer*, provider for God's house or church, only makes sense when we realise that he means by the church the poor, *die armen menschen*, whom God had created and in whom God dwells.[39] Luther's identification of the congregation with the commune, the socio-political entity, rather than with the traditional parish marked a very significant shift. Frequently it is impossible to know whether the reference is to the community as a social or an ecclesiastical entity, and this is itself highly significant, of course. The concerns of the 'Church' embrace the totality of local life.

The Church is community, and preaching, pastoral care, the administration of Baptism and the Lord's Supper must build up community. Wolfgang Musculus, representative of many 'second-level' Reformers, was anxious to remove any images around the altar, because they created a barrier between pastor and people

[37] '"Iusticia, Teutonice fromkeyt." Theologische Rechtfertigung und bürgerliche Rechtschaffenheit. Ein Beitrag zue Sozialgeschichte eines theologischen Konzepts', in *Die frühe Reformation in Deutschland als Umbruch*, pp. 307–33.

[38] *Underweisung etlicher artickel*, 1525, fol. Cii, quoted in Chrisman, *Conflicting Visions*, p. 189.

[39] *Von der neuen Wandlung*, in Laube, *Flugschriften der Bauernkriegszeit*, p. 556/9ff.

when the Eucharist was celebrated.[40] At the rural level, on the other hand, change was slow. The new, university-trained, married pastor was often seen as working on behalf of a centralising court and could be suspect as an interfering outsider. In the cities, particularly in the early years, one is struck by the new partnership between preaching pastor and literate laity[41] but, as Abray suggests for Strasbourg, there was a growing tendency to accept the clerics as the experts on theological matters to whom one deferred.[42]

It may also be, as feminist historians unanimously conclude, a more male Church, and a more male vision of God. Mary is missing, the female saints are missing, though the use of the Virgin Queen of heaven to keep ordinary women in their place has to be remembered in this context. We are still finding our way towards a just assessment of this very complex question.

We do know that as the Reformers' imaginations began to falter, as intransigent resistance and cruel circumstance ground them down, pessimism crept in: the recognition, as Hans Sachs said, that the Word of God could be preached forever, but the wealthy would never change their ways.[43] One way of dealing with this was by increasing resort to legislation. Another was by projecting their frustration on to Jew, *Schwärmer*, pope or witch. The new song became flattened into a propaganda chant for confessional purposes. The window of opportunity for women, and therefore men, was slammed shut; the Utopian dreams of the artisans and others for a less hierarchical society; the gut-wrenching cry for truth, for justice, for freedom; all were suppressed with that special imaginative skill reserved for frightened élites. And

---

[40] '*damit ich altar, sacrament und das volk alles vor mir habe*'. *Wolfgang Musculus (1497–1563) und die oberdeutsche Reformation* (ed. Rudolf Dellsperger, Rudolf Freudenberger and Wolfgang Weber; Berlin: Akademie Verlag, 1997), p. 144.

[41] Lay people would listen to the preacher but consult their own copy of Scripture, coming back with questions, and expecting a right to be heard; cf. Chrisman, *Conflicting Visions*, esp. pp. 123, 160–9.

[42] Abray, *The People's Reformation*.

[43] Chrisman, *Conflicting Visions*, p. 193.

yet again, if we will, not suppressed if we dare to revisit them. No hack is as cheap as a historian who becomes a cynic. As Pelikan has finely said, by including the dead in the circle of our discourse, we at least enrich the quality of the conversation.[44]

When a friend heard that I planned a series of lectures on the Protestant imagination, she replied, disconcertingly: 'And how do you propose to ascertain what that is?' It is true that we cannot get beyond the thin trail of material and written evidence. We cannot drag back the Old Testament Reformer, Luther, or the New Testament Reformer, Jacob Hutter, and put them on the therapist's couch to reveal their inner souls. We have to respect the final hiddenness of people's inner motivations, dream-worlds and prayer life.

At times such as ours, on the cusp of a new millennium, the historian in us, looking back at the Other in the past, merges with the seer in us, peering into the shape of the future. Merges too, of course, with the carer and lover in us, reaching out to the hurt and wistfulness of our present, very fragmented, time, when those who hold the levers to power politically, economically and culturally act as if modernity were all, although the theorists trip around the periphery dancing to the rhythms of post-modernism.

It is my hunch that part of our difficulty is that the Reformation does offer us the menace of real hope, but by way of a gritty determination, such as Argula von Grumbach illustrates, to face the theatre of real life, not to pretend it is an enchanted one. To face up, like the Psalmist whom Luther loved so much, to the existentials, the experiences of loss, failure and suffering, but somehow to discover the music and the lyrics surfacing out of these depths as the new song. Nothing heroic or promethean about this courage; quite the opposite, for it is given only in the abyss. The *solo Christo* resonates through it all.

Walter Benjamin talked about the creation of space, the suspension of history, the seizing of the critical moment. Part of the imaginative shift of the Reformation was to critique the

---

[44] Jaroslav Pelikan, *The Vindication of Tradition*, p. 81.

enchanted world, to point to the fragmentary, allusive, veiled nature of our access to divinity, to teach us to be content with hints and wistfulness (a better word for eschatology); but another part of it, in Edwin's Muir's words with which we began, was to appreciate the fabulous and mysterious character of our humanity, pointing beyond itself to the grace at the heart of the universe. We don't understand much; let us act passionately on the little that we do.

BIBLIOGRAPHY

Primary

Personenselekt Cat. 110 (Grombach), Bayerische Haupstaats-archiv, Munich.

BRANT, SEBASTIAN, *Das Narrenschiff.* Ed. H. A. Junghans and Hans-Joachim Mähl. Stuttgart: Reclam, 1964.

The Essential Carlstadt. Fifteen tracts by Andreas Bodenstein (Carlstadt) from Karlstadt. Tr. and ed. E. J. Furcha. Waterloo, Ontario and Scottdale, PA: Herald Press, 1995.

Flugblätter der Reformation und des Bauernkrieges. 50 Blätter aus der Sammlung des Schloßmuseums Gotha. Ed. Hermann Meuche. Catalogue by Ingeburg Neumeister. Leipzig: Insel-Verlag, 1976.

Flugschriften der Bauernkriegszeit. Ed. Adolf Laube, Hans Werner Seiffert. Berlin: Akademie-Verlag, 1975.

Flugschriften der frühen Reformationsbewegung (1518–1524). Ed. A. Laube, A. Schneider and S. Loos. 2 vols, Berlin, 1983.

Flugschriften des frühen 16. Jahrhunderts. Ed. H. J. Köhler, H. Hebenstreit and C. Weismann. Zug, 1978–87.

The German Peasants' War. A History in Documents. Ed. and tr. Tom Scott and Bob Scribner. New Jersey: Humanities Press, 1991.

Die historischen Volkslieder der Deutschen (5 vols, Leipzig, 1865–96). Ed. Freiherr Rochus von Liliencron.

Luther's Works. Ed. J. Pelikan and H. Lehman. 55 vols, Philadelphia and St Louis: Concordia, 1955ff.

D. *Martin Luthers Werke.* Kritische Gesamtausgabe. Weimar, 1883ff.

Thomas Müntzer: Schriften und Briefe. Ed. Günther Franz. Gütersloh: Gerd Mohn, 1968.

The Collected Works of Thomas Müntzer. Tr. and ed. Peter Matheson. Edinburgh: T. & T. Clark, 1988.

Quellen zur Geschichte des Bauernkrieges. Ed. Günther Franz. Darmstadt: Wiss Buchgeselleschaft, 1963.

SACHS, HANS, *Die Wittenbergisch Nachtigall.* Ed. Gerald H. Seufert. Stuttgart: Reclam, 1974.

Lazarus Spengler Schriften, Band 1 (1509–23). Ed. Berndt Hamm and Wolfgang Huber. Quellen und Forschungen zur Reformationsgeschichte, 61. Gütersloh: Gütersloher Verlagshaus, 1995.

Vom Christlichen abschied aus diesem tödlichen leben des Ehrwirdigen Herrn D. Martini Lutheri. Drei zeitgenössische Texte zum Tode D. Martin Luthers. Mit einer Einführung von Peter Freybe . . . und einem Nachwort . . . von Siegfried Bräuer. Stuttgart: Verlag Joachim W. Siener, 1996.

Argula Von Grumbach. A Woman's Voice in the Reformation. Ed. and tr. by Peter Matheson. Edinburgh: T. & T. Clark, 1995.

Secondary

ABRAY, LORNA JANE, *The People's Reformation. Magistrates, Clergy and Commons in Strasbourg 1500–1598.* Oxford: Basil Blackwell, 1985.

BÂLE, EMILE, *Religious Art from the Twelfth to the Eighteenth Century.* Princeton: Princeton University Press, 1982.

Walter Benjamin's Philosophy. Destruction and Experience. Ed. Andrew Benjamin and Peter Osborne. London and New York: Routledge, 1994.

BIELFELDT, DENNIS, 'Luther, Metaphor and Theological Language'. *Modern Theology* 6:2 (1990), pp. 121–35.

BLICKLE, PETER, *The Revolution of 1525. The German Peasants' War from a New Perspective.* Tr. Thomas A. Brady, Jr., and H. C. Erik Midelfort. Baltimore and London: Johns Hopkins University Press, 1981.

BOSSY, JOHN, *Christianity in the West, 1400–1700.* Oxford: Oxford University Press, 1985.

BRADSTOCK, ANDREW, *Faith in the Revolution. The Political Theologies of Müntzer and Winstanley.* London: SPCK, 1997.

BRADY, THOMAS, *Turning Swiss: Cities and Empire, 1450–1550.* Cambridge Studies in Early Modern History. Cambridge University Press, 1985.

BRUEGGEMANN, WALTER, *Texts Under Negotiation. The Bible and the Postmodern Imagination.* Minneapolis: Fortress Press, 1993.

BURKE, PETER, *Popular Culture in Early Modern Europe.* Aldershot: Scolar Press, 1994.

CHRISMAN, MIRIAM USHER, *Conflicting Visions of Reform. German Lay Propaganda Pamphlets, 1519–1530.* Atlantic Highlands, NJ: Humanities Press, 1995.

Convents Confront the Reformation: Catholic and Protestant Nuns in Germany. Ed. Merry Wiesner-Hanks; tr. Joan Skocir and Merry Wiesner-Hanks. *Reformation Texts with Translation: Women of the Reformation, vol. 1.* Milwaukee: Marquette University Press, 1996.

Die frühe Reformation in Deutschland als Umbruch. Wissenschaftliches Symposium des Vereins für Reformationsgeschichte 1996 (Schriften des Vereins für Reformationgeschichte Nr. 199). Ed. Bernd Moeller, with Stephen E. Buckwalter. Gütersloh: Gütersloher Verlagshaus, 1998.

DIPPLE, GEOFFREY, *Antifraternalism and Anticlericalism in the German Reformation. Johann Eberlin von Günzburg and the Campaign against the Friars.* Aldershot: Scolar Press, 1996.

DIXON, SCOTT C., *The Reformation and Rural Society. The Parishes of Brandenburg-Ansbach-Kilmbach 1528–1603.* Cambridge Studies in Early Modern History. Cambridge, 1996.

DUFFY, EAMONN, *The Stripping of the Altars: Traditional Religion in England c. 1400–1580.* New Haven and London: Yale University Press, 1992.

FABIAN, JOHANNES, *Time and the Other: How Anthropology Makes its Object.* New York: Columbia University Press, 1983.

FRAENGER, WILHELM, *Jörg Ratgeb. Ein Maler und Märtyrer aus dem Bauernkrieg.* Dresden: VEB Verlag der Kunst, 1972.

FRAZIER, CHARLES, *Cold Mountain.* New York: Grove-Atlantic, 1997.

FUDGE, THOMAS A., '"The Crown" and the "Red Gown": Hussite Popular Religion', in *Popular Religion in Germany and Central Europe 1400–1800,* pp. 38–57. Ed. Bob Scribner and Trevor Johnson. London: Macmillan, 1996.

GENTILCORE, DAVID, *From Bishop to Witch. The System of the Sacred in Early Modern Terra d'Otranto.* Manchester and New York: Manchester University Press, 1992.

GLEASON, ELISABETH G., *Gasparo Contarini. Venice, Rome and Reform.* Berkeley, Los Angeles and Oxford: University of California Press, 1993.

GOERTZ, HANS-JÜRGEN, 'Adel versus Klerus. Antiklerikale Polemik in Flugschriften des Adels', in *Antiklerikalismus und Reformation.* Göttingen, 1995.

HAIGH, CHRISTOPHER, *Reformation and Resistance in Tudor Lancashire.* London: Cambridge University Press, 1975.

HALBACH, SILKE, *Argula von Grumbach als Verfasserin reformatorischer Flugschriften.* Europäische Hochschulschriften. Series XXIII Theology: vol. 468. Frankfurt am Main, 1992.

HEXTER, J. H., 'Utopia and Geneva', in *Action and Conviction in Early Modern Europe: Essays in Memory of E. H. Herbison.* Ed. T. K. Robb and J. E. Siegel. pp. 77–89. Princeton: Princeton University Press, 1969.

HOBAN, RUSSELL, *Riddley Walker.* London: Pan, 1992.

HOLL, KARL, *Gesammelte Aufsätze zur Kirchengeschichte.* 7th edition. Tübingen: J. C. B. Mohr, 1948.

HUIZINGA, JOHAN, *The Autumn of the Middle Ages.* Chicago: University of Chicago Press, 1996.

Hutten, Müntzer, Luther. Werke in zwei Bänden. Ed. Siegfried Steeler. Berlin Weimar, 1982.

The Image and the Book. Iconic Cults, Aniconism and the Rise of Book Religion in Israel and the Ancient Near East. Ed. K. van der Toorn. Leuven: Peeters, 1997.

JENS, WALTER, *Zueignungen. Literarische porträts.* Munich: Piper, 1962.

KOESTLER, ARTHUR, *The God that Failed: Six Studies in Communism.* London: Hamish Hamilton, 1950.

KÖPF, ULRICH, 'Die Bilderfrage in der Reformationszeit.' *Blätter für Württembergische Kirchengeschichte* 90 (1990), pp. 38–65.

LÉVI-STRAUSS, CLAUDE, *The Raw and the Cooked. Introduction to a Science of Mythology.* Tr. John and Doreen Weightman. London: Jonathan Cape, 1970.

LOWENTHAL, DAVID, *The Past is a Foreign Country.* Cambridge: Cambridge University Press, 1985.

MCKEE, ELSIE ANNE, *The Writings of Katharina Schütz Zell.* Vol I *Interpretation*; vol. II *A Critical Edition.* Leiden: Brill, 1998.

'Man weiss so wenig über ihn'. Philipp Melanchthon. Ein Mensch zwischen Angst und Zuversicht. Ed. Evangelisches Predigerseminar Lutherstadt. Wittenberg: Drei Kastanien Verlag, 1997.

MARTI, KURT, *Zart und genau. Reflexionen Geschichten Gedichte Predigten.* Ed. Siegfried Bräuer and Hansjürgen Schulz. Berlin: Evangelische Verlagsanstalt, 1985.

MATHESON, PETER, 'Whose Scripture? A Venture into Reformation Hermeneutics.' *The Mennonite Quarterly Review* LXX (April 1996), pp. 191–202.

——, 'A Reformation for women? Sin, grace and gender in Argula von Grumbach.' *Scottish Journal of Theology* 49/1 (1996), pp. 39–56.

——, *The Rhetoric of the Reformation.* Edinburgh: T. & T. Clark, 1998.

——, 'The Cornflower in the Wheatfield. Freedom and Liberation in Thomas Müntzer.' *Archive for Reformation History* 89 (1998), pp. 41–54.

METZ, JOHANN BAPTIST, *Faith in History and Society.* London: Burns & Oates, 1980.

MOELLER, BERND, *Imperial Cities and the Reformation.* Tr. and ed. H. C. Eric Midelfort and Mark Edwards, Jr. Philadelphia: Fortress, 1972.

MOXEY, KEITH, *Peasants, Warriors and Wives. Popular Imagery in the Reformation.* Chicago and London: University of Chicago Press, 1989.

MUIR, EDWIN, *An Autobiography.* London: Hogarth Press, 1954.

NEWMAN, J. H., *An Essay on the Development of Christian Doctrine.* Harmondsworth: Penguin, 1974.

OBERMAN, HEIKO A., *Masters of the Reformation: The Emergence of a New Intellectual Climate in Europe.* Tr. Dennis Martin. Cambridge, 1981.

——, *The Impact of the Reformation.* Edinburgh: T. & T. Clark, 1994.

OZMENT, STEVEN, *When Fathers Ruled. Family Life in Reformation Europe.* Harvard University Press, 1983.

OZMENT, STEVEN, *Magdalena and Balthasar. An Intimate Portrait of Life in 16th century Europe Revealed in the Letters of a Nuremberg Husband and Wife* . . . New York: Simon & Schuster, 1986.

——, *Three Behaim Boys. Growing up in Early Modern Germany.* New Haven and London: Yale University Press, 1990.

PACKULL, WERNER O., *Hutterite Beginnings: Communitarian Experiments During the Reformation.* Baltimore and London: Johns Hopkins University Press, 1995.

PELIKAN, JAROSLAV, *The Vindication of Tradition.* New Haven and London: Yale University Press, 1984.

PIANZOLA, MAURICE, *Bauern und Künstler. Die Künstler der Renaissance und der Bauernkrieg von 1525.* Tr. Tilly Bergner. Berlin: Henschelverlag, 1961.

PRESS, VOLKER, 'Wilhelm von Grumbach und die deutsche Adelskrise.' *Blätter für deutsche Landesgeschichte.* Vol. 113 (1997), pp. 396–431.

Protestant History and Identity in Sixteenth Century Europe. Vol. 2, *The Later Reformation.* Ed. Bruce Gordon. Aldershot: Scolar Press, 1996.

The Pursuit of Holiness in Late Medieval and Renaissance religion. Ed. Charles Trinkaus and Heiko A. Oberman. Leiden: Brill, 1974.

Reformation in Nürnberg. Umbruch und Bewahrung. (Schriften des Kunstpädagogischen Zentrums im Germanischen National-museum Nürnberg, 9.) Nuremberg: Verlag Medien & Kultur, 1979.

RIEGER, GEORG, *Das Leben Argulae von Grumbach gebohrner von Stauffen als einer Jüngerin Jesu, Zeugin der Warheit und Freundin Lutheri* . . . Stuttgart: Metzler & Erhardt, 1737.

ROPER, LYNDAL, *Holy Household: Women and Morals in Reformation Augsburg.* Oxford: Oxford University Press, 1991.

ROTHKRUG, LIONEL, *Religious Practices and Collective Perceptions: Hidden Homologies in the Renaissance and Reformation.* (Historical Reflections, Vol. 7), 1980.

SCOTT, TOM, *Thomas Müntzer. Theology and Revolution in the German Reformation.* London: Macmillan, 1989.

——, 'The Communal Reformation between Town and Country', in *Archiv für Reformationsgeschichte. Sonderband: Die Reformation in Deutschland und Europa: Interpretation und Debatten*, pp. 175–92. Ed. Hans R. Guggisberg and Gottfried G. Krodel. Gütersloh: Gütersloher Verlagshaus, 1993.

SCRIBNER, BOB, *Popular Culture and Popular Movements in Reformation Germany.* London: Hambledon Press, 1987.

STAYER, JAMES, 'Die Anfänge des Schweizerischen Täufertum im Kongregationalismus.' *Umstrittenes Täufertum, 1525–1975. Neue Forschungen.* Ed. Hans-Jürgen Goertz. Göttingen: Vandenhoeck & Ruprecht, 1975.

——, *The German Peasants' War and Anabaptist Community of Goods.* Montreal and Kingston; London and Buffalo: McGill-Queen's University Press. 1991.

STEWART, ALISON, 'Paper Festivals and Popular Entertainment. The Kermis Woodcuts of Sebald Beham in Reformation Nuremberg.' *Sixteenth Century Journal* XXIV/2 (1993), pp. 301–50.

VEIT, PATRICE, 'Private Frömmigkeit, Lektüre und Gesang im protestantischen Deutschland der frühen Neuzeit: das Modell der Leichenpredigten', in *Frühe Neuzeit – Frühe Moderne? Forschungen zur Vielschichtigkeit von Übergangsprozessen.* Ed. Rudolk Vierhaus. Veröff. d. Max-Planck-Instituts für Geschichte, 104. Göttingen: Vandenhoeck & Ruprecht, 1992.

WANEGFFELEN, THIERRY, *Ni Rome ni Genève. Des Fidèles entre deux chaires en France au XVIe siècle.* Paris: Honoré Champion, 1997.

WHITING, ROBERT, *The Blind Devotion of the People: Popular Religion and the English Reformation*. Cambridge: Cambridge University Press, 1989.

WIESNER, MERRY E. *Gender, Church and State in Early Modern Germany*. London and New York: Longmans, 1998.

WILLIAMS, G. H., *Wilderness and Paradise in Christian Thought; the biblical experience of the desert in the history of Christianity and the paradise theme in the theological idea of the university*. New York: Harper, 1962.

WINK, WALTER, *Engaging the Powers: Discernment and Resistance in a World of Domination*. Minnesota: Fortress Press, 1992.

Wisdom and Wit. An Anthology from the Writings of Gordon Rupp. Ed. John A. Vickers. Peterborough: Methodist Publishing House, 1993.

WUNDERLI, FRITZ, *Peasant Fires: the Drummer of Niklashausen*. Bloomington, IN: Indiana University Press, 1992.

INDEX OF NAMES AND PLACES